Elaine Connell has a degree in English, History and Politics from Manchester Metropolitan University, an MA in English from the University of Salford and a teaching certificate from the University of Manchester.

She has been teaching English for 20 years and has worked for the Open University, for the Manchester Metropolitan University and a variety of schools and colleges in West Yorkshire. She is currently a Senior Examiner in English for a leading exam board.

Her fascination with the life and work of Sylvia Plath goes back over twenty years and was the subject of her MA thesis. She maintains a fascinating forum about Sylvia Plath on the Internet at

http://www.hebdenbridge.co.uk/plath

Elaine Connell started writing in the mid-eighties. Her first published work was in the *Eight to Late* (Overdue Books) anthology of women's writing. In 1987, she was awarded a Yorkshire Arts bursary for new writers.

Since then, she has contributed to *News on Sunday*, the *Guardian* and the *Yorkshire Post*. In 1991, *Cycling in Search of the Cathars*, (Pennine Pens) a travel history book on southwest France, which she wrote with Chris Ratcliffe, was published.

Published 1993 by Pennine Pens
Reprinted1995
Second Edition 1998
Copyright © Elaine Connell
All rights reserved

ISBN 1 873378 01 7

Typeset and published by Pennine Pens.
32, Windsor Road, Hebden Bridge,
West Yorkshire, HX7 8LF. Tel/Fax 01422-843724
books@penpens.demon.co.uk
http://www.hebdenbridge.co.uk

SYLVIA PLATH

KILLING THE ANGEL
IN THE HOUSE

by

Elaine Connell

Pennine Pens

For my father,
Ted Connell,
who also took his own life

and

In memory of
Maureen Lea,
a great Spirit and a true teacher

CONTENTS

Preface to the
Second Edition

When I completed this book in 1993 I ended the last chapter with the assertion that it would certainly not be the last attempt to explain and illustrate the enigma and paradox which Plath represents. However, almost as soon as I'd written those words I began to question whether there was really much else to write when it seemed to be that nearly all the facets of her life, times and work had been so exhaustively covered by many scholars, journalists and biographers.

In January 1998, her former husband Ted Hughes stunned the literary world with the completely unexpected publication of *Birthday Letters* a poetic account of his relationship with Sylvia Plath. This reawakened the controversy surrounding the poets provoking new areas of discussion on each of their lives and literary achievements.

Eager to hear what others thought about Hughes' new collection and any new light it might shed on Sylvia I started a **Sylvia Plath Forum** on the Internet. This has proved to be far more successful than we could ever have anticipated and remains a very stimulating arena in Plath Studies. It has definitely confirmed my original statement that Plath invites repeated attempts to read and elucidate her work and to account for her life and death.

Contributors to the Forum, who have mainly been Americans, have given me many new ideas for further research on Plath and much useful new information which may well provide the basis for another book. It is a fine example of how the Internet can be used for excellent, high quality debate and discussion, bringing together people with similar interests who might never have made contact except for its existence.

Although there have been many excellent postings to the Forum I should like to thank and acknowledge in particular Stewart Clarke, Melissa Dobbs, Jack Folsom and Peter Steinberg for their regular, incisive and perceptive offerings both to the Forum itself and in the form of e-mails to me. The last year has certainly demonstrated the value of the new technology and the exciting possibilities which it offers to scholarship.

Birthday Letters is some of the best work Hughes has done in years. It ranks with his early poems which many people, including myself, had always preferred and which of course he wrote in the early years of his relationship/marriage with Sylvia. It is almost as if remembering and reflecting upon her has rekindled the full range of his genius again.

Even the title of the collection derives from Plath as it is an almost direct allusion to Sylvia's "Poem For A Birthday", the long poem in her first collection *Colossus* which, at the time, marked a change in direction in her poetry. It was her first unambiguously autobiographical work and represented a new departure in her writing, much as *Birthday Letters* denotes a new development in Hughes' poetry. He leaves his usual territory of the consciousness of animals, mythological figures and deranged individuals to speak directly about his own life and the centrality of his marriage to Plath. This is the first time he's written about himself such a personal and open style.

I read *Birthday Letters* through in one sitting and found it an interesting, rewarding and emotional experience. Here was a strongly physical portrayal of a Sylvia who no-one else has ever conjured up quite so vibrantly. We are given cinematic, powerful images of her charismatic attraction. Her height (the bane of her life according to her Journals) which she feared was so unappealing is lovingly portrayed as graceful and compelling:

> *Swaying so slender*
> *It seemed your long, perfect, American legs*
> *Simply went on up.*

The descriptions of each part of her body and they way they moved:

> *long, balletic, monkey-elegant fingers, the face*
> *- a tight ball of joy, the African-lipped,*
> *laughing, thickly/Crimson painted mouth,*
> *eyes.......a crush of diamonds*

are startling evocations of a breathing, animated Sylvia which the camera has failed to capture in quite the same way Hughes has. They are also suffused with a sense of a much missed eroticism.

Plath's status as a stranger in a strange land is also a major theme of this collection. From Hughes' joyful echoing of Donne's famous line: *Oh my America, my new found land* in:

> *My new world.*
> *So this is America, I marvelled.*
> *Beautiful, beautiful America*
>
> "18, Rugby St."

to his reports of her longings for her own country found in "Stubbing Wharfe" and "You Hated Spain", the reader is constantly reminded of the huge differences between the USA and Europe which existed in the 50's and 60's and how very alien Plath must have felt in her adopted country.

By the end of the book I found myself crying both for the tragedy of the premature loss of a great poet and for the great sense of the deeply passionate love whose passing Hughes obviously regrets to the point of lamentation:

The house made newly precious to me
By your last lonely weeks there, and your crying.

I peered awhile, as through the keyhole,
Into my darkened, hushed, safe casket
From which (I did not know)
I had already lost the treasure.
                                        "Robbing Myself"

Birthday Letters reinforced the opinion first expressed in Chapter Nine of this book that the marriage was by no means completely over when Plath committed suicide and that their five or six months' separation had not obliterated all of Hughes' love for her. I am pleased that five years ago I distanced myself from the facile tendency so many people have of needing to find someone else to blame for a suicide's actions.

This inclination towards accusation shows the power of the taboo which still surrounds suicide. People who are otherwise tolerant, liberal and thoughtful on most social issues display a knee-jerk reaction where self murder is concerned. This demonstrates how far as a culture we still have to go in breaking the suicide taboo.

Hughes' accounts of the reaction of Frieda and Nicholas to their mother's loss are almost too painful to read for someone like myself who has also lost a parent to suicide, but they reveal a man touched by great tragedy who has been struggling with its legacy for many years. I now feel much more certain that his refusal to talk about Plath for so many years may well be the product of this heritage and his desire to protect his children from further harm.

His account of Plath's life and death also illustrate a factor I touched upon in this book's biographical Chapter One, the tendency of unresolved grief in children to manifest itself in later life in the form of depression, anger and the development of an overly demanding personality. All of these personality traits are frankly yet lovingly exposed in Sylvia throughout the collection. Hughes also displays a deep grasp of the nature of the psychic wound that Otto Plath's premature and unnecessary death inflicted upon his daughter.

Hughes also touches on the mystical in the poem "St. Botolph's" which deals in some depth with their respective astrological charts. A central tenet of the book seems to be that Hughes believes Plath was fated to die as she did and he could also be suggesting that her natal chart had a large part in it. Of course, those of us who more sceptically believe that: "The fault lies in ourselves, not in our stars" can dismiss this as special pleading via mumbo jumbo but it might well have been an explanation which Sylvia herself would have accepted given her shared belief with Hughes in astrology and psychic powers.

Of course, *Birthday Letters* only represents Hughes' own story of his fateful marriage. But for the past thirty five years we have only had Sylvia's and mainly accusatory biographers' and critics' reports of their life together.

His affair with Assia Wevill and subsequent separation from Sylvia were undoubtedly major factors in the depression which led to her death. It is therefore understandable that many people hold him responsible for robbing us all of a major poetic talent, but he is not necessarily the "vampire" or "Man in black with a Meinkampf look" in life that he has become in poetic myth.

Many women have experienced their husbands' adultery and single parenthood without resorting to suicide. The roots of Sylvia's suicide go much deeper than the breakdown of her marriage to Hughes and *Birthday Letters* is a perceptive, though possibly partial illustration of some of the forces which pushed her towards her fate.

My only reservation about his treatment of her suicide is that there are no traces of the countless "if onlys" which usually haunt those left behind.

As a feminist, I remain convinced that the social forces which shaped Plath played a far greater role in her life, work and death than most critics have given them credit for. From my discussions with Jack Folsom via the Internet, I feel I have gained even further insight into the socially oppressive conventionality of 1950's American society which was particularly critical for women. The force of this pressure to conform was apparently even greater than I stated in my chapter on the 1950's.

Because of her background and possibly her personality type, Sylvia was an insecure girl and young woman who strived to fit in at all costs, even when this conformity ran so completely counter to her true creative nature and aspirations. For those of us who were young adults in the 60's and 70's when radicalism and individuality were so prized it can be hard to imagine just what it was like to reach maturity during the 1950's.

The ambivalence and rage we find in Plath's work is not merely the product of mental illness or personality disorder but one way of responding to living during a time which labelled women with artistic or career ambitions as unfeminine or unnatural. To live so permanently at odds with the mores of one's culture requires a degree of personal strength and resilience which Sylvia, already bearing the weight of unresolved grief from her father's death and seething with anger from the breakdown of her relationship with Hughes, did not possess.

On the Sylvia Plath Forum, several contributors have criticised this using of her personal experience and her attempt to formulate a personal mythology from the events of her life. They have seen it as rather narcissistic and self-centred reducing her work to mere confession rather than something which is applicable to us all. But what is mythology itself but the attempt of people over time to make lasting stories and meanings out of the major events of their personal experiences? It doesn't matter that someone takes a scene from their own life and invests it with mythological significance because it is from these very scenes that mythology originates.

Those of us who try to emphasise the mythological roots of Plath's work as I do in Chapter Eight of this book are probably trying to rescue it from the charge that it is merely the product of some neurotic's overactive, if not mad, mind. Those of us engaged in literary criticism remain profoundly influenced by the Eliot/Pound dictum on the necessity for impersonality in poetry and this stress on Plath's use of mythology makes her oeuvre conform. I am coming to the conclusion that we should perhaps just reject that particular model and claim Plath for the transcendent subjectivism of the Romantics.

I also can't help but notice that if a woman uses her own experience in her art she is readily viewed as deranged or solipsistic; but a man using the same technique (such as Lowell for example) is interpreted as speaking for the human condition through the vehicle of his own life.

Many of the contributions to the Sylvia Plath Forum have attested to how much Plath speaks for Everywoman - possibly one of the few times this has occurred in literature (with due acknowledgement to Anne Bradstreet). Certainly, it may be the first time that threatening female anger has been portrayed in all its terrifying force expressed by an identifiable individual woman and not a character such as Clytemnestra or Medea. Perhaps the problem is that Everyman still can't fully understand, or is reluctant to contemplate, the rage which lurks so much in the female psyche. This book remains an attempt at clarification of that peculiarly female anger and its socio-cultural roots which Sylvia Plath did so much to illuminate.

Elaine Connell
September 1998

Preface to the
First Edition

Every so often in the middle of an argument about the relative merits of female equality, someone, usually male, would point to the lack of great women artists. After he'd been answered with the Brontes, Virginia Woolf and George Eliot, he'd reply somewhat scathingly, "Oh novelists! But there's no real artists. Where are your poets and playwrights?"

For some time I had no answer. I couldn't think of a single woman poet or dramatist. I'd certainly not come across them in my undergraduate study of English and Politics.

In my late teens, I had become interested in feminism. Like many other young women in the sixties and early seventies, I found my ideas and life transformed by the rise of the contemporary Women's Movement. Through my interest in feminism, I came to hear about an American poet, Sylvia Plath. When I learned of her suicide, my fascination grew. My father had gassed himself in 1966 and I wanted to gain some insight into the mental state of someone who had also committed suicide. I eagerly sought out her work and was immediately captivated by its power, the violent, compelling imagery and the fact that she'd made taboo subjects such as menstruation, childbirth, pregnancy and breastfeeding into haunting poetry.

For a time I could see why some feminists were claiming Plath as a forerunner of the feminist movement. Parts of her poetry and virtually the whole of her only novel, *The Bell Jar*, provided witty, lucid and penetrating insights into patriarchy. Indeed, Plath has frequently been described as a "contemporary feminist icon". (*Sunday Times* 16th February 1992)

Much as I wanted to claim Plath as a feminist writer, the more I began to study her, the more I began to realise that feminist was an adjective I could never use as an overall description of her work. There were too many contradictions in it. For example, she seemed to believe that masochism was an essential and defining attribute of female personality: "Every woman adores a fascist" (*Daddy*) and her hostility to other women was at times anti-feminist. She seemed to see her situation as fixed and unchangeable, which is the antithesis of feminism.

One of the most fundamental principles of the Women's Movement has been the idea of *sisterhood* rather than competition between women. Another has been the belief that society can be changed. In several seminars on Plath, other feminists have argued that Plath is an essentially feminine poet. They have pointed to her search for an ultra-masculine man, her emphasis on childbearing as a necessary experience for women and, most damningly of all, her caricaturing of other women as either evil rivals, mindless morons or frigid spinsters. Such images conform very closely to some of the more popular stereotypes of femininity in Western culture.

This book is the result of my struggles with what I still feel is the enigma of Sylvia Plath. However, it is this very quality of elusiveness which I feel is one of the major attractions of her work.

The book grew out of my M A. thesis which I presented to the Department of Modern Languages at the University of Salford in 1990. I should like to thank and acknowledge the supervisor of that thesis, Barry Wood, who also suggested the title.

My ideas about Sylvia Plath have been germinating for many years. Consequently, one of my acknowledgments goes back a long time. I should like to thank Jeff Wainwright of Manchester Metropolitan University whose teaching in the 1970's on Plath's work was always so perceptive and stimulating.

Louise Parkinson provided me with useful and interesting comments on the manuscript. Thanks to the long suffering staff of Hebden Bridge Library, especially Irene Hughes and Karen Spence whose tact and patience are seemingly limitless!

I owe a special thanks to my partner Chris Ratcliffe who not only took over the running of our household and the care of our son Morgan during the writing of first the thesis, and then the book, but also made many valuable comments on the manuscript, designed and edited the book, and did a substantial part of the typing.

INTRODUCTION

*"It is as if she were some collective halluci-
nation - a Lourdes miracle or an apocalyptic
horsewoman - momentarily illuminating
the landscape for some, darkening it for
others, and leaving behind her an audience
furiously divided between apostles and
infidels...... Sylvia Plath is the centre of a
Holy War."*

Harriet Rosenstein [1]

There can be few poets or writers who have been as controversial as Sylvia Plath. Writing from the most unconventional edge of the human psyche, Plath entices her readers into an angry, grief-stricken, emotional maelstrom whose existence many would prefer to deny. Her poetry has been called 'extremist' and the disputes which have raged since her death certainly deserve this label. The list of contrasting adjectives applied to her work have been endless: 'feminine', 'feminist', 'schizoid', 'sane', 'rational', 'irrational'.

A major focus of debate has been within feminist literary criticism and concerns how we are to classify Plath. After all, the poet who warned men to:

Beware
Beware
Out of the ash
I rise with my red hair
And I eat men like air
                    Lady Lazarus

is the same poet who claims that all women are innately masochistic:

Every woman adores a Fascist,
The boot in the face, the brute
Brute heart of a brute like you.
                    Daddy

One of the problems in this debate has been a rather obvious one. Commentators have used the words *feminist* and *feminine* without ever defining them. It is as if everyone knows what we mean when we use these terms. But too often they're being used in a Humpty-Dumptyish fashion meaning precisely what the users wish them to mean.

The dictionary tells us that to be feminine is to "have the qualities ..... proper to women," [2] while a feminist is an "advocate of political, economic and social equality for women". [3] But each of these definitions lacks precision so perhaps it is worthwhile to work towards a more exact definition.

To be feminine in our society is to be dependent, submissive, passive, masochistic, unselfish and accommodating oneself at all times to the needs of men and children. It is to regard marriage, and especially motherhood, as the highest possible fulfilment in life. And perhaps above all, it is to be 'nice'. Traditionally, femininity is associated with nurturing and the development of the emotions rather than the intellect.

In addition to advocating the political, social and economic equality of women, a feminist is a woman who locates the source of women's oppression in the patriarchal system for which men are held responsible. A feminist feels anger and defiance against this system and realises the necessity of joining with other women in sisterhood to overcome it. Feminists do not necessarily reject either men or childbearing but wish to abolish the restrictions on self-development which attachment to men and the rearing of children currently entail.

How do these definitions apply to Plath? By selective quotation from her poetry, one could construct a case for using either term to describe her work. On the feminine side, there is the woman who celebrates the god/beast/man for whom submission by the woman is a Lawrentian ecstasy.[4] The woman who derides intellectualism in other women and elevates the sensual feminine principle[5] is obviously no feminist. Worst of all, from a feminist perspective, is the cry that we have already heard: "Every woman adores a fascist". What better example of feminine masochism could we wish for in an attempt to claim Plath for traditional femininity?

And yet, it is the same poet who writes so defiantly of previously taboo subjects in poetry. Plath has given literature superb evocations of menstruation and breast-feeding. Her powerful, unsentimental images of childbirth could never be interpreted as submissively feminine. She also creates a specifically female hell where:

> there's a stink of fat and baby crap
>
> *Lesbos*

numbed by the occasional:

.....pill to kill
The thin
Papery feeling
                  Cut

Neither of these images conform to the essential feminine quality of niceness.

Similarly, Plath displays a strong antipathy towards men, especially in her later poems which contain statements any radical feminist of the early 1980's could have made. There are almost prophetic similarities between Plath's assertion that men are to blame for all the horrors of modern civilisation:

> There was something about them like
> cardboard and now I had caught it
> That flat, flat, flatness from which ideas,
> destructions
> Bulldozers, guillotines, white chambers of
> shrieks proceed.
>   *Three Women*

and the way in which contemporary feminists have drawn parallels between war, violence, extreme right-wing ideologies and traditional male behaviour.

The major contemporary feminist dictum that "the personal is political" and therefore worthy of analysis is also foreshadowed in her work. When the Women's Movement began in the late '60's, Plath was adopted by it as an almost prophetic goddess of feminism.

In historical and possibly even contemporary terms, this adoption was understandable and perhaps inevitable. In the '60's and '70's, most of the work literature students studied was by male authors. The discovery of any good woman writer was so rare that she immediately became a female 'hero'.

There was a great temptation to overreact to at last finding a writer with whom one could identify. These female 'heroes' can give validations of our own anxieties and the sense that we are not alone in our feelings. This point is perhaps the crucial factor in understanding the function of women writers for women themselves. Quite often the literary value of a book or its philosophical agenda becomes secondary in comparison to the value of discovering a writer from whom we are not alienated on the grounds of our sex and what that means for our experience of the world.

However, when the poems collected in *Winter Trees* and *Crossing The Water* were published in 1971, some feminists began to criticise her attitude towards other women. Others pointed out that her extreme individualism was incompatible with a feminist label. Harriet Rosenstein, quoted at the beginning of this chapter, was moved to call this disagreement within the Women's Movement a 'Holy War'.

Perhaps what Rosenstein calls the apostles and the infidels in this argument are both wrong. The faults in both interpretations lie in the fact that they have taken Plath and her work out of its historical context of the '50's and early '60's and read her poems as if they had been written in the late '60's and early '70's.

Throughout her poetry, Plath demonstrates a vacillation between feminine and feminist stances to such an extent that neither word can be satisfactorily applied to her writings.

Plath's work is that of an artist working towards defining herself as a woman and discovering an authentic, female, poetic voice in a culture which placed the creative woman in a contradictory and conflicting situation. Her poetry cannot be definitively used, as it has been in the past twenty years, as a weapon in an ideological battleground.

What Plath has written reveals a woman torn between the traditional feminine sphere of submission to men, devotion to children, elevation of motherhood and the development of a fiercely independent creative female self whose "blood jet is poetry"[6] rather than the "blood jet" of menstruation or childbirth.

This conflict and Plath's attempt to build a valid poetic identity was one of the mainsprings of her artistic achievement. It grew out of the society which shaped her as both a woman and poet. There are few critical commentaries on Plath which have made more than a passing reference to the society in which she was reared, lived and subsequently died. I hope that this book will go some way towards remedying this deficiency.

Whether or not Plath was a feminist, she was certainly affected by the era in which she lived. In her book, *The Feminine Mystique*, Betty Friedan, an American contemporary, provides an illuminating perspective on the society which produced Sylvia Plath. This work describes the years which immediately preceded the birth of the Women's Movement. From Friedan's analysis of the 1950's we can see the profound effect that the prevailing ideology of female dependency and domesticity had upon women of that time.

Plath's life and work demonstrate the profound tensions endured by an exceptionally intelligent and creative woman coming into maturity in a society which denied a full place to the female artist.

Another important aspect of Sylvia Plath's art, which has been neglected by many other writers with the exception of Judith Kroll, is the role the mythology of the

Great Goddess played in her art. From the time when she met Ted Hughes this mythology played an important part in shaping Plath's work. After their separation, it was to continue in providing her with a basis for reconstructing a valid female poetic identity.

Much of the recent work about Plath has tended to concentrate on her life to the relative exclusion of her work. Indeed, some of the speculation and publicity surrounding her life and death has been more appropriate to a star from *Dynasty* than to one of the most important poets of the twentieth century.

Obviously, understanding of the often, intensely personal material, which she wrote towards the end of her short life is aided by biographical knowledge. But appreciation of Plath has been as much impeded by the stress on her life as it has been aided. How many of those who read the sensational accounts of her tragedy actually go on to read her poetry?

Although I will provide a brief biography and occasionally refer to it throughout the book, my emphasis will be on the poems and her novel rather than the person.

CHAPTER ONE
BIOGRAPHY

Sylvia Plath was born in Boston, Massachusetts on 27th. October 1932. There was a large age-gap between her parents. Otto Plath, her father, was twenty years older than her mother, Aurelia. They had met at Boston University where he was a Professor of Botany and Entomology and she was a postgraduate student completing a Master's degree.

When Sylvia arrived, Otto declared that all he needed was a son born in two and a half years' time. With chilling accuracy, on 27th. April 1935, exactly two and half years later, Warren Plath was born. Professor Plath's colleagues toasted him as "the man who gets what he wants, when he wants it". [1]

This getting of what he wanted carried on throughout the rest of his life. According to Aurelia Plath, household life was almost entirely centred around the needs of Otto and his work.[2] Perhaps marriage to a man who was old enough to be her father, who held a good position in a respected university and had been her teacher, naturally led to Aurelia Plath becoming an obedient wife. She certainly provided the young Sylvia with a role model of female compliance within marriage, even though she maintains that it was difficult for her to subdue her own personality as much as Otto required:

> At the end of my first year of marriage, I realised
> that if I wanted a peaceful home - and I did - I

would simply have to become more submissive, although it was not my nature to be so. [3]

Otto was a leading authority on bees and wrote a book, *Bumble Bees And Their Ways,* which became the standard academic treatise on the subject. Aurelia has described how she felt under constant pressure to keep her children quiet so that he could work. This preoccupation with his work made him a somewhat distant father.

Sylvia, an intelligent girl, soon learned that the most certain way to gain his attention was by academic prowess. Consequently, she became a high achiever at school. At the age of seven, her first poem was published in a local newspaper.

In 1936, the year after Warren's birth, Otto became unaccountably ill. He could not accept weakness in himself and went to great lengths to carry on with his teaching and writing. In addition to bringing up their two small children, Aurelia now helped him enormously in the preparation of his classes. Under the pressure of this illness his distance from the children increased even more. Often, he was so weak that he could only see them for twenty minutes a day. In one sense Sylvia can be said to have grown up with scarcely any effective fathering.

Otto refused to visit a doctor because he feared that he had cancer. He had seen a close friend and colleague die of lung cancer and did not want to go the same way. In fact, he had diabetes which would have been treatable if he had sought medical advice earlier.

Diabetics have poor circulation and are therefore susceptible to serious illnesses resulting from comparatively minor accidents. In the summer of 1940, Otto stubbed his little toe against his bureau. Later in the day, the toe had turned black and extensive bruising developed up into the rest of his leg. Aurelia, who had been unsuccessfully trying for some time to persuade him to seek medical advice, called in their doctor who immediately diagnosed diabetes.

Otto's leg subsequently developed gangrene and had to be amputated at the thigh on October 12th. Following the operation he developed pneumonia and he died almost one month later, on 5th. November 1940, from an embolus on his lung.

If he had consulted a doctor earlier his diabetes could have been treated and his premature death avoided. The surgeon who amputated his leg was astounded by the case and demanded to know, "How could such a brilliant man be so stupid?"[4] When Sylvia was told about his death she declared that she was never going to speak to God again.

In the twentieth century, Western society has become inadequate at dealing with death and grief. Medical advances have made the loss of parents in childhood a far rarer occurrence than it was in previous centuries. Therefore, those children who are bereaved find that their experience is at worst unacknowledged, or at best, ineptly handled as an emotional issue. In the way in which they handled their loss, the Plath family seem to have been fairly typical examples of this cultural inadequacy.

Aurelia felt that she needed to put on a brave face for her children. Even when she told them of Otto's death she did not cry in their presence. She herself had been terrified by seeing her mother crying when she'd been a small child and believed that by suppressing her emotions she was sparing her children further pain. Later in life, Sylvia was to accuse her mother of having shown no grief at her husband's death. This accusation is understandable as Sylvia and Warren were allowed no time to grieve. Sylvia went to school as normal on that day. The children neither saw their father's body nor attended his funeral. [5]

Recent studies on death and grief have demonstrated that failure to mourn can cause grave psychological problems in later life. Common effects are the development of an 'angry' personality, emotional insatiability and fear of further loss.

We can obviously see major traces of these features in Plath's life. Her adult depressions and the recurrent use of the imagery of her father's loss can be interpreted as a consequence of this lack of expression of overt mourning within her family.

The bereavement also plunged the Plaths into serious financial difficulties. Because he did not trust insurance salesmen, Otto was not adequately insured. Aurelia was forced to move in with her parents. Sylvia, who loved the sea, now lived inland. She experienced this as yet another loss in her life and realised that it was to provide her with future rich material for her poetry, the sea is a constant presence in her work:

> My father died, we moved inland. Whereon those
> nine first years of my life sealed themselves off
> like a ship in a bottle - beautiful, inaccessible,
> obsolete, a fine, white flying myth. [6]

In the following years, Aurelia worked tremendously hard as a teacher in order to support the family.

Sylvia carried on being a brilliant student. Even in her high school days, she regarded herself as a writer and treated her ambitions in a very professional way. She obtained a full scholarship to Smith, one of America's most prestigious Ivy League colleges where she was very successful. Her work also aroused the interest of a rich, successful writer, Olive Higgins-Prouty who became Sylvia's patron.

In 1953, at the end of her third year at Smith, she won a prize which involved spending the summer working for the women's magazine, *Mademoiselle,* in New York.

When she returned home to discover that she had not obtained an expected place on a writing course, she began to sink into a depression where she could not work, learn or sleep. Her mother, realising that her daughter was ill, persuaded her to see a psychiatrist. This psychiatrist administered unanaesthetised ECT which, in addition to being a horrific experience, did not lift her out of depression.

On August 24th 1953, after leaving a note to her mother saying that she was going for a long walk, Sylvia went to the cellar of her home. Hiding herself in a crawl space underneath the living room she took an overdose of sleeping pills; and remained unconscious in the cellar for two days.

Meanwhile, Mrs. Plath had reported her disappearance and a police search was instituted. Both local and national media became involved and headlines such as "Brilliant Smith Girl Missing" were printed on the front pages of newspapers. Sylvia was discovered two days later by her brother Warren when he went down into the cellar and heard her moaning.

When Sylvia reached the emergency room of Newton-Wellesley Hospital, a nurse said that she was "more dead than alive." [7] She spent several months in a mental hospital and was treated with ECT again: this time under anaesthetic.

Eventually, Sylvia became the patient of a young woman psychiatrist. Dr. Ruth Beuscher, the mother of four children, seemed to provide the role-model Plath so desperately needed of a woman who was combining femininity with an intellectual, independent life.

February 1954 saw her return to Smith and ultimate graduation with the highest honours. This was followed by a Fulbright scholarship which enabled her to go to Cambridge University to read English.

Throughout Sylvia's life, relationships with men were difficult. Her diaries and her autobiographical novel, *The Bell Jar* reveal a young woman who feared she would never find a satisfactory and fulfilling relationship. One man is rejected because he is smaller than she is, another because he cannot appreciate poetry, and yet another because of the conventional views he holds on women's role.

At Cambridge, she met and fell in love with the poet Ted Hughes who she described as "very simply the only man I've ever met whom I could never boss." [8] For all her intelligence and creativity, she was typical of her era in that she needed a man to be, or appear to be, her superior.

Sylvia Plath and Ted Hughes married in 1956. In its early years, their marriage seems to have been an exceptionally strong and artistically fruitful partnership. Both benefited enormously from their relationship. Sylvia typed and marketed Hughes' work assiduously and professionally. Ted provided her with new ideas and insights about the world. He also inspired her with a great deal of confidence about her poetic identity.

Hughes had been interested in the mythology of the Great Goddess for some years and it is likely that it was he who introduced Plath to the philosophy of the sacred feminine which so profoundly affected the rest of her work.

In the Autumn of 1957, Plath returned to America with Hughes where she took up a job as a lecturer at Smith while Hughes lectured at the University of Massachusetts. Plath was apparently a conscientious, popular and successful teacher. However, like so many writers who had gone before her, she found that teaching robbed her of the nervous energy needed for writing. Teaching English was particularly frustrating for, as she wrote to her brother Warren on 5th. November 1957,

> I am sacrificing my energy, writing and versatile intellectual life for grubbing over 66 Hawthorne papers a week and trying to be articulate in front of a rough class of spoiled bitches.... How I long to write on my own again! When I'm describing Henry James' use of metaphor to make emotional states vivid and concrete, I'm dying to be making up my own metaphors. [9]

Ted also found that teaching interfered with his literary ambitions. During the following year they gave up their posts, took a variety of undemanding part-time jobs and devoted a considerable amount of time to their poetry. However, Ted could not settle in the States and in 1960 they went back to England. Plath, who had experienced some difficulties in conceiving, was delightedly pregnant with their first child.

By this time, Hughes had received recognition as a major new poetic talent. His first collection, *The Hawk In The Rain,* won the Harper's Poetry Award in 1956 and was published amidst great critical acclaim in 1957. Sylvia had actually entered Hughes for the prize. It's likely that without her constant pushing of his work as well as her own, Hughes would probably have taken far longer to achieve fame as a poet.

At the same time as Ted was enjoying this fame, Sylvia was receiving many rejections. Her first collection, *Colossus,* had been published but had received only muted approval. She was to remain in Hughes's poetic shadow for the rest of her life.

Plath and Hughes' daughter, Frieda Rebecca, was born on 1st April 1960. Plath was an enthusiastic and loving mother but the next two to three years were dogged by illness and stressful events. In 1961, she had a miscarriage followed by an appendectomy. In May of that year she became pregnant again with her third child and the family moved to a large, dilapidated vicarage in Devon.

The birth of her son, Nicholas Farrar, in January 1962 appears to have been a watershed in the marriage of Plath and Hughes. Her diaries and letters of the period seem to be one long complaint about the problems of combining motherhood and poetry. Following her father's interest, Plath also took up bee-keeping.

In 1962, Hughes began an affair with Assia Wevill, the wife of another poet. Plath was distraught. When Dorothea Krook, Plath's Cambridge tutor in Moral Philosophy, had seen Plath's rapture with her marriage in its early days, she had experienced a rather eerie intuition about its future consequences:

> I remember at least once experiencing a thrill of fear at the idyllic pitch and intensity of her happiness, What would happen (I said, or half-said to myself) if something should ever go wrong with this marriage of true minds? ....Yet if, inconceivably, it should, she would suffer terribly. I held my breath to think how she would suffer. [10]

Krook proved to be right in her premonition. Any marriage break-up is traumatic for the partners but Sylvia perhaps experienced hers more intensely because of the early loss of her father. In many ways, Hughes was a father figure for her as well as a husband.

Perhaps this high pitch of emotional intensity in the Plath/Hughes marriage was what led to several desperate and distressing incidents in the early stages of his affair with Assia. Plath's suspicions about her had been denied by Hughes for some time. Consequently, if Sylvia answered when she phoned, Assia would pretend to be a man. After one of these calls, Sylvia became so enraged by the deception that she pulled the telephone loose from its wires. Soon after this, Hughes left.

Two months later, in December, Plath decided to go and live in London. Devon now seemed too isolated from literary and intellectual life. Whilst house-hunting in London, she was delighted to find a flat in a house which had once been occupied by Yeats.

Both Plath and Hughes believed that she had psychic gifts. What followed on her return to Devon to pack lends credence to this idea. She took down her *Collected Plays of Yeats,* opened it at random and used her finger to select a message from the poet (another believer in psychic powers). Her finger fell upon the lines:

> Get wine and food to give you strength and courage
> and I will get the house ready.

She was delighted by this 'message' and prepared for her move to London with apparent gusto. Although still distressed by Ted's infidelity, she seems to have greeted her new life with a positive attitude.

However, once more she was plagued by her own and the children's illnesses. An added stress was that she was also coping with one of the coldest winters in living memory. England's climate, and the fact that there were none of the comforts of America such as central heating to be able to cope with it, had been one of her recurrent grievances about her adopted country. Several bouts of 'flu and constant emotional stress led to a large weight loss. All of these problems were exacerbated by the incessant demands of looking after small children, with only intermittent help.

In the midst of all this, she wrote her most memorable poetry: some critics have called it poetry by which future generations will seek to know us. To write these poems she rose at 4 a.m. and worked until her children woke up.

Her doctor, who was treating her with anti- depressants, thought that her mental state was improving. However, one of the unfortunate consequences of these drugs is that they may lift a depressive out of a state of inactivity and indecision. Before the long term anti-depressant effect occurs, the result may well be suicide. On 11th. February 1963, Sylvia Plath gassed herself. She was thirty years old.

Plath had made a second suicide attempt in 1962 when she'd driven her car off the road. One of her poems, 'Lady Lazarus', indicates that she had a notion that every decade she had to dice with death in order to be reborn. There is convincing evidence that her suicide was one of these dicings with death which went wrong, rather than a fully foolproof attempt.

The night before her death she'd gone to borrow stamps from Trevor Thomas, the tenant in the flat below, a man with whom she normally had little contact. She asked him detailed questions about the time he got up in the morning. It seems almost as if she was checking that he would be awake and smell the gas, or be woken up by the nurse who was due to arrive at 9 a.m. next morning.

She ensured that Frieda and Nicholas were not harmed by opening their bedroom window and surrounding the door with newspapers. Food and milk were also left out for them. As far as it is known, there was no note except one which said, "Please call Dr. Horder" and gave the number of her doctor. This seems a strange thing to do for someone fully intent on self-destruction.

Unfortunately, as coal gas is heavier than air, the fumes sank through the floorboards stupefying the other tenant. He did not wake up when the agency nurse arrived at 9 a.m. The nurse didn't get into the house until 11 a.m. by which time Sylvia was dead. If she'd managed to enter the house at nine as planned, there is a good chance that Sylvia might have survived. She had lost her third gamble with death.

CHAPTER TWO
THE 1950'S

"The time is out of joint, oh cursed spite,
That ever I was born to set it right."
Hamlet

Sylvia Plath grew up in a society plagued by economic depression and a war which ended with the explosion of an atomic bomb. Even though her poetry isn't overtly political, she was very aware of these contemporary events and conscious of how they affected her work.

Her early adult life was shaped by the prosperity of the America of the 1950's. Except for the witch-hunts of supposed Communists, American society in this decade was socially and ideologically inert. It was dominated by a conservatism which led even a recognised and successful male poet like Robert Lowell into feelings of depression:

> These are the tranquillised *Fifties,*
> And I am forty.
> *Memories of West Street and Lepke*

If such an era could produce cynicism in a relatively established forty year old poet, it was to prove an even more impossible time for an unknown female poet in her twenties from a far more modest social background than Lowell's.

Betty Friedan's seminal feminist tract, *The Feminine Mystique*, was based on research she had conducted in the 1950's with women of Plath's age. She paints a bleak picture of the life which most women of these years were leading.

She believes that the traumas of the Second World War had made people desperate for security and the familiar. One of the consequences of this was the relegation of women into the home and the elevation of domesticity as the most fulfilling and only desirable role for them.

The dilemma for an educated young woman like Plath was particularly acute. She was given the opportunity to develop intellectually on the tacit understanding that her intelligence would not be used outside the home. According to Friedan, this dichotomy produced an atmosphere of stultification and boredom within American colleges. As one of her interviewees said:

> They know they're not going to use their education. They'll be wives and mothers......
> It's a disappointment to know you're going to stop now. [1]

A report on the attitudes of women in the prestigious Vassar College in 1956 discovered that even the most able women of this generation were intent on a domestic future:

> Strong commitment to an activity or career other than that of housewife is rare....Few plan to continue with a career if it should

conflict with family needs.... As compared to the 'feminist era' few students are interested in the pursuit of demanding careers. Similarly, one finds few instances of people like Edna St. Vincent Millay, individuals completely committed to their art by the time of adolescence and resistant to any attempts to tamper with it.[2]

This 'feminine mystique' was also given the stamp of scientific validity by the mass popularisation of Freudian psychology. Peter Blos's influential study, *On Adolescence*, which was published at the same time as Friedan's book, epitomises the 1950's American thinking on women and the family:

> It is the prerogative of the female to display her physical charms.....Her need is to be loved. The boy is permitted only to display what he can do; he therefore focuses his pride on prowess and accomplishment. His attainments may lie in athletic, intellectual, academic, sexual, occupational or creative endeavours. Daring, perseverance, speed and power are the attributes considered masculine, which can be displayed publicly by the male. [3]

In its turn, this type of thinking led to the suspicion that a woman who desired commitment to work or art was not only exceptional but also 'unnatural'!

> The feminine mystique, elevated by Freudian theory into a scientific religion, sounded a simple, overprotective, life-restricting, future-denying note for women. Girls who grew up... almost independent enough, almost resourceful

enough, to meet the problems of the fission-fusion era, were told by the most advanced thinkers of our time to go back... And their own respect for the authority of science... kept them from questioning the feminine mystique. [4]

A promising poet and successful student like Plath was faced with equally unsatisfactory choices in her life. Choosing to have a career meant sexual inactivity and no children, whilst choosing marriage and motherhood meant having little other real fulfilment.

In *The Feminine Mystique,* Betty Friedan gives a moving account of her own personal dilemma when she won a much prized graduate doctoral fellowship at Smith:

> I came to a frightening dead end in my own vision of the future..... "Is this what I really want to be?" .... I felt the future closing in - and I could not see myself in it at all. I had no image of myself stretching beyond college. ......I had begun to know who I was and what I wanted to do. I could not go back now. I could not go home again, to the life of my mother and the women of my town.....But now that the time had come to take the deciding step, I suddenly did not know what I wanted to be.
>
> ....I lived in a terror of indecision for days, unable to think of anything else.... We walked in the Berkeley hills and a boy said: "Nothing can come of this, between us. I'll never win a fellowship like yours.".... I gave up the fellowship.[5]

Friedan's sense of being paralysed about what she wanted to do with her life is almost a mirror image of the crisis experienced by Esther, the *Bell Jar's* heroine.

Esther has a vision of the future in which various roles are laid tantalisingly before her and she is unable to choose any of them. Like Friedan, Plath's heroine is affected by the cultural notion that intellectual achievement and sexual fulfilment are irreconcilable goals for women.

On their Commencement Day at Smith, Plath and her contemporaries were addressed by America's most radical politician, Adlai Stevenson. Even such a leading reformer as this told the assembled women that their generation's future was to be "wives and mothers."

Many women of the 1950's seem to have welcomed this future happily:

> We loved it even if it seemed to hurl us back to
> the satellite role we had escaped for four years -
> second class citizens in a man's world where our
> only possible achievement was a vicarious one. [6]

There was tremendous social pressure to conform to this satellite role and Plath at many times seemed to long to do so. Anne Stevenson's account of Plath's life, whilst flawed in many respects, seems accurate when she discusses how the poet longed to be 'ordinary'.[7] Being ordinary in the context of the 1950's meant a happy marriage, husband and children. In her journals, letters and work, Plath is always striving for this goal in spite of her regular insight into its impossibility for an intelligent and creative woman. For example, in June 1959, she feared that she could not have children and wrote in her journal:

> I have worked, bled, knocked my head on
> walls to break through to where I am now.... I

want a house of our children, little animals, flowers, vegetables fruits. I want to be an Earth Mother in the deepest richest sense. I have turned from being an intellectual, a career woman: all that is ash to me.

.....I have come with great pain and effort, to the point where my desires and emotions and thoughts center around what the normal woman's center around. [8]

Ed Cohen, Plath's pen pal during her early adult life, had warned her about the trap she was setting for herself when he wrote:

You can have your career, or you can raise a family. I should be extremely surprised you can do both within the framework of the social structure in which you now live. [9]

Unlike Cohen, Plath did not seem able to see herself as part of a social structure or historical process. Indeed, she seemed to see the conditions of the 1950's as the permanent one for women. One perceptive acquaintance, quoted by Nancy Hunter-Steiner, saw this as the root of her problems:

... she seemed certain that Syl would be happier if she weren't constantly torn between her impulses, and the set of values she had acquired from society... Sylvia could not guess that society would ever change; she seemed to see the taboos and tension of her background as permanent conditions that could never be substantially altered; and she bore them with surface resignation. [10]

It is not surprising that Plath saw herself as an exception, or even as a freak amongst women. In her book, *Women Of Ideas,* Dale Spender has demonstrated how successive waves of feminism throughout history have been ridiculed, then partially accommodated by society and ultimately eliminated from intellectual and historical consciousness. As she comments:

> ....why didn't I know about all the women of the past who have protested about male power is that patriarchy doesn't like it. These women and their ideas constitute a political threat and they are censored. By this means women are kept in the dark, with the result that every generation must begin virtually at the beginning, and start again to forge the meanings of women's existence in a patriarchal world....every fifty years women have to reinvent the wheel. [11]

Spender analyses the 1950's as a particularly fallow time for feminism. She has found very little evidence of women addressing the problems of living within the patriarchy during that decade. She suggests that during this time

> the taboos against any expression of these ideas on the part of women or men may have been greater than in other recent decades. [12]

Unless one accepts the idea that Plath was suffering from mental illness from her childhood, then the depth of despair found in her work can be very difficult to understand. Throughout her life, Plath was inexorably drawn towards the image of happy, maternal fulfilled womanhood which was the dominant ideology of 1950's society. However, she was also an intelligent, ambitious woman whose creative compulsion rendered her incessantly at odds with the way in which her society defined women.

Given her isolation from feminist foremothers, her lack of historical perspective and her seeming inability to appreciate the possibility of social change, she saw her situation as fixed and even archetypal. In such circumstances, the hyperbolic extremism of her poetry and a desire for personal annihilation is an almost rational response.

Her repeated use of the imagery of concentration camps, fascism, torture and the identification of herself as a Jew/victim also becomes more comprehensible when it is viewed in this light. Just as the death camps operated as closed, inhuman societies where one's race defined one's future, so American society of the 1950's inhumanly defined a person's life by their sex.

A woman who either could not, or would not, conform to the feminine role was tortured by doubt, loneliness and appalling psychiatric treatment, such as the unanaesthetised ECT administered to Plath during her mental breakdown. We cannot, of course, compare the situation of women in the 50's completely with that of the Jews in the camps. The feeling of rage and powerlessness is, I believe, comparable.

Many Jewish survivors of the concentration camps have told how they identified with their tormentors rather than their fellow victims. Much of Plath's poetry contains an image of herself as a victim/survivor, enraged at her plight, but wishing to become as powerful as the men who oppress her. It is also interesting that she chose to kill herself by gas when she had enough sleeping pills to poison herself. Like the Jews, she was gassed and, like them, we can see her as a human sacrifice to a particular epoch.

In one sense, Plath is a contemporary female Hamlet; born into a time and circumstances in which what society demands of her runs completely contrary to her inner self. The stresses of this condition are well illustrated in her autobiographical novel, *The Bell Jar.*

CHAPTER THREE
THE BELL JAR

Plath's only published novel, *The Bell Jar*, is set in the New York of summer 1953. It recounts the story of Esther Greenwood, a brilliant, creative college student who has won a guest editorship on the staff of a national women's magazine. Although she is aware that her society dictates that she should be ecstatically happy, Esther feels lost and alienated. The novel, which charts her decline, fall and 'rebirth' is directly drawn from Sylvia's own summer at *Mademoiselle;* her suicide attempt, hospitalisation and recovery.

The opening lines of *The Bell Jar* closely relate the heroine's personal dilemma and impending mental breakdown to the political situation of 1950's America.

> It was a queer, sultry summer, the summer they electrocuted the Rosenbergs, and I didn't know what I was doing in New York. ....I couldn't help wondering what it would be like, being burned alive all along your nerves. [1]

The Rosenbergs were Jewish victims of McCarthyism who were falsely accused of being Russian spies. Plath captures the Cold War atmosphere of a society which executed this innocent couple, whose only 'crime' was that they had been members of the American Communist Party. Esther, a thinly disguised version of Plath herself, goes on to demonstrate in a series of desperately funny and intense images what this type of society did to women.

Whilst Esther is involved in rejecting major aspects of the American 1950's she seems incapable of envisaging any other way to live. She has internalised her society's values at the same time as being at odds with them. She is the All-American Girl living out the American Dream of rags to riches by individual effort. This dream has no personal relevance but Esther is haunted by the fact that it retains its social significance:

> I was supposed to be having the time of my life. I was supposed to be the envy of thousands of other college girls just like me all over America......And when my picture came out in the magazine the twelve of us were working on - drinking martinis in a skimpy, imitation silver-lamed bodice stuck on to a big, fat cloud of white tulle, on some Starlight Roof, in the company of several anonymous young men with all-American bone structures - everybody would think I must be having a real whirl.
>
> "Look what can happen in this country," they'd say. "A girl lives in some out of the way town for nineteen years so poor she can't afford a magazine, and then she gets a scholarship to college.... and ends up steering New York like her own private car."
>
> Only I wasn't steering anything, not even myself. [2]

Esther feels dehumanised in this milieu, describing herself as "like a numb trolley-bus." She is unable to integrate the worlds of academic and artistic achievement with what her society defines as social success for women.

In the first third of the novel she compares herself to three other women who seem to represent three possible feminine identities for her. She envies each their particular quality: Doreen's sophisticated, socially experienced and sexually uninhibited life, Betsy's ordinariness with its acceptance of "normal" femininity and Jay Cee's successful career. However, simultaneous with her envy is her perception of the unsatisfactory nature of their lives.

Doreen is a cynical dilletante with little purpose in her life who is also implicated in Esther's denouncement of her rich contemporaries:

> ...they had just graduated from places like Katy Gibbs and were secretaries to executives and junior executives and simply hanging round in New York waiting to get married to some career man or other. These girls looked awfully bored to me......Girls like that make me sick. [3]

But at the same time as she pours scorn on this female type she is pulled towards it for she admits that she feels "so jealous I can't speak". [4]

In contrast to Doreen, Betsy is very wholesome:

> They imported Betsy straight from Kansas with her bouncing blonde pony tail and Sweetheart of Sigma Chi smile. [5]

She also achieves success in the most traditionally

feminine way by becoming a model. This conformity is rejected by Esther when she maliciously enjoys Doreen's spiteful nickname for Betsy, 'Pollyanna Cowgirl'.

But it is probably Esther's doubts about Jay Cee, the editor of the magazine, which are the most fundamental blow to her vision of her own future. Jay Cee is a successful career woman but she is seen as almost inevitably unattractive and incapable of a full sexuality:

> I tried to imagine Jay Cee out of her strict
> office suit and luncheon duty hat and in bed
> with her fat husband, but I just couldn't do it. [6]

Doctor Nolan, Esther's psychiatrist, provides a role model of an attractive, sexual and intelligent woman, but in comparison to the other women in the novel she seems to lack reality. As Pauline Bennett comments:

> The picture Esther draws of her has an almost
> movie-star ring. Dr. Nolan steps out of a film
> from the late forties, fancy spectacles and all. [7]

The men in Esther's life also provide little help in the problem of how she is to live. Her boyfriend, Buddy Willard, is the typical 'All-American' boy, even down to his name which borders on caricature. Buddy, is Plath's portrayal of a young man who is the ideal 1950's husband. Esther's childhood sweetheart, a medical student from a 'good', educated, religious family; he also holds all the 'correct' American conventional attitudes.

This very eligibility is counterbalanced by his insensitive nature and the fact that Esther finds him sexually repulsive. This insensitivity and repulsiveness is graphically described in one of the novel's funniest scenes in which Buddy reveals his nakedness to Esther for the first time:

> I stared at Buddy while he unzipped his
> chino pants and took them off and laid them on
> a chair and then took off his underpants that
> were made of something like nylon fishnet.
> "They're cool," he explained, "and my mother
> says they wash easily."
> Then he just stood there in front of me and I
> kept on staring at him. The only thing I could
> think of was turkey neck and turkey gizzards
> and I felt very depressed. [8]

Esther meets more exciting men at a UN party but the simultaneous translator, Constantin, is impotent and the diplomat, Marco, is an inveterate misogynist.

Esther finally loses her virginity to Irwin, a college professor, but the event closely resembles rape. There is little pleasure in it and the haemorrhage which follows carries an implication that sexual experience drains a woman's life blood.

Esther cannot find any answers to her difficulties in personal relationships because her problem is intrinsically a social one. Female intelligence and creativity were completely irreconcilable with the conventional female stereotype of the 1950's. Esther does not initially perceive the social roots of her crisis but sees herself afflicted with a mere inability to make decisions about the future. She has a vision of the future in which she starves to death amidst plenty because she cannot make a choice:

> I saw my life branching out before me like the
> green fig tree in the story. From the tip of every
> branch, like a fat, purple fig, a wonderful future
> beckoned and winked. One fig was a husband
> and a happy home and children, and another fig

was a famous poet and another fig was a brilliant professor....I saw myself sitting in the crotch of this fig tree, starving to death, just because I couldn't make up my mind which of the figs I would choose. I wanted each and every one of them, but choosing one meant losing all the rest. [9]

Plath is showing through her heroine that she apprehended the notion of the impossibility of women having work, artistic, sexual and domestic fulfillment as men can. The feminine mystique of the 1950's prevented most women from questioning why they could not lead well-rounded lives. It is against this attitude to femininity in her social background that Esther revolts most strongly.

Within the novel, 1950's truisms about women's role are spoken by Esther's mother and Mrs. Willard. They, however, are obviously only convenient vehicles for expressing what Plath saw as the general social climate. Mrs. Willard, Buddy's mother, has renounced her own life to become an efficient wife and mother.

...cook and clean and wash was just what Buddy Willard's mother did from morning till night, and she was the wife of a university professor and had been a private school teacher herself. [10]

This woman's definition of fulfilment is typical of the social climate:

...his mother said, "What a man wants is a mate and what a woman wants is infinite security... What a man is is an arrow into the future and what a woman is is the place a man shoots off from [11]

49

Esther refuses to accept this definition of femininity as being applicable to herself. When she imagines herself as a wife she depicts a life of unceasing drudgery, totally unsuitable for an intellectual:

> This seemed a dreary and wasted life for a girl with 15 years of straight A's, but I knew that was what marriage was like. [12]

When her mother presses her into learning shorthand to prepare her for the traditional women's world of work she rapidly rejects it:

> The trouble was, I hated the idea of serving men in any way. [13]

She is, however, still seeing this hatred as her own pathological problem, referring to it as a 'trouble'. There seems a sense here that this is how life is and that it is impossible to change male and female roles. One of the book's most compelling similes occurs when Esther compares marriage and motherhood to:

> being brainwashed, and afterwards you went about numb as a slave in some private, totalitarian state. [14]

In spite of these almost feminist political recognitions of the reality of marriage and maternity in the 1950's, Esther still craves 'normality'. She is deeply attracted to motherhood and is fascinated by Dodo Conway, the mother of several children who is portrayed in archetypal Earth Goddess terms:

A serene, almost religious smile lit up the woman's face. Her head tilted happily back, like a sparrow egg perched on a duck egg, she smiled into the sun. [15]

Immediately after she has been observing Dodo's fecundity Esther is struck by the sterility of her own life:

I crawled back into bed and pulled the sheet over my head. But even that didn't shut out the light, so I buried my head under the darkness of the pillow and pretended it was night. I couldn't see the point of getting up. I had nothing to look forward to. [16]

She also expresses a desperate desire for female social responsibility and orthodoxy just before her suicide attempt:

I was thinking that if I'd had the sense to go on living in that old town I might just have met this prison guard in school and married him and had a parcel of kids by now. It would be nice living by the sea with piles of little kids and pigs and chickens. [17]

Babies recur both externally and as images throughout the novel. Often they are images of horror and death but also ones of regeneration and creativity. For example, after she receives treatment by insulin coma, Esther becomes a baby herself:

I fanned the hot milk out on my tongue as it went down, tasting it luxuriantly, the way a baby tastes its mother. [18]

Betty Friedan has written that she began to be interested in feminism when she observed that she and her friends were deeply unhappy even though they possessed everything their culture told them that a woman needs. She named this sense of dissatisfaction with life "the problem that has no name." Plath's *Bell Jar* reads like an individual's experience of this problem. Esther summarises her own social and mental dilemmas most accurately when she replies to Buddy's proposal and more or less names the problem:

> ...if neurotic is wanting two mutually exclusive things at one and the same time, then I'm neurotic as hell. [19]

Under such pressures, life itself becomes as hollow as the society's expectations and alienation grows to such an extent that Esther repeatedly compares herself and others to objects.

Esther's recovery is achieved through self-acceptance and her overt rejection of the idea of a fixed biological destination for women. She gains this partly by comparing herself favourably with other women she has previously envied:

> I thought how sad it was Joan looked so horsy... And Dee Dee's husband was obviously living with some mistress or other. [20]

But the largest step forward for Esther is a more explicitly feminist one: her sense of freedom when she is fitted with a contraceptive:

> I climbed up on the examination table thinking:
> "I am climbing to freedom, freedom from fear,

freedom from marrying the wrong person like
Buddy Willard, just because of sex." [21]

Of all the conflicts experienced in *The Bell Jar*, the
issues surrounding babies are not resolved. Even when
Esther has become "her own woman" she distrusts her
emotions towards children.

> How easy having babies seemed to the women
> around me! Why was I so unmaternal and apart?
> Why couldn't I dream of devoting myself to baby
> after fat puling baby like Dodo Conway? [22]

On the subject of children, Esther always questions
herself rather than asking questions about what makes
having children so difficult in her society. Finally, she
adopts a compromise. She ignores the situation of most
women, and her involvement in it, to attempt to build an
independent life in isolation. Perhaps, however, this was
the largest measure of self-definition possible for a
woman of that time. These conflicts were to recur in her
poetry because they were incapable of an individual
solution.

CHAPTER FOUR
MEN

The predominant image of men which Plath presents in her poetry is of violent, controlling, omnipotent, highly sexual, but emotionally flat figures who possess a rage for order and rationality. Her attitude towards men wavers between intense love and equally intense loathing, archetypal feminine responses and feminist perceptions of the way in which men control the world and thereby dehumanise it for all.

The early poems, 'Pursuit' and 'Ode to Ted', are archetypally feminine in the way in which they celebrate the god/beast/man for whom submission by the woman is ecstasy.

The poem 'Pursuit' was written immediately after Plath's first meeting with Ted Hughes. The heroine is being hunted by a panther who lives on the blood of women. Early in the poem, the reader becomes aware that the panther and the pursuit are actually a metaphor for men and their sexual relationship with and power over women. There is a strong sense of masochism within the psyche of the woman which demonstrates that she is actually enjoying the chase at the same time as she realises that the panther will ultimately destroy her.

In 'Pursuit', the use of a panther to represent a man invests him not only with the beauty and energy of the animal but also its destructive, death-bringing powers.

While Plath admits that "one day I'll have my death of him", throughout the poem she describes him in exalted and magical terms. He is

> more lordly than the sun....
> ......His voice waylays me, spells a trance.

She perceives that submission to this man "compels a total sacrifice" and yet while she runs from him she seems to be always looking back to see that "he keeps my speed" and is filled with excitement rather than fear.

This poem seems to represent the desire to be sexually consumed by a superior, more than man figure. While it is a glorification of male sexual power over women, it is significant that Plath depicted man in non-human terms. Just as the male Romantic poets painted an image of woman in ethereal, impossibly ideal, Nature-goddess terms, so Plath seems to be creating a similarly impossible Romantic image of man as god, beast and destroyer of a willing womankind:

> Kindled like torches for his joy
> Charred and raven women lie.

Hughes studied Anthropology at Cambridge and was fascinated by the practice of shamanism within tribal societies. The poem has decided echoes of shamanic practices and initiation rites within it. One of the shaman's powers is that he can appear to be an animal. One of his functions is to perform the initiation ceremony for young men. This often takes the form of a journey through a wilderness or forest where the young man is tested by the shaman who reveals nature to him. Through the experience of this journey, the boy confronts himself and emerges as a man.

'Pursuit' seems like a female initiation ceremony. Plath begins the poem with a quotation from Racine:

Dans le fond des forets votre image me suit.

(In the depths of the forests your image follows me)

Just as tribal male initiation ceremonies take place in dense forests so does this one. The initiation into womanhood seems to involve running from an inescapable fate:

Insatiate, he ransacks the land
Condemned by our ancestral fault;
He eats, and still his need seeks food,
Compels a total sacrifice.

These lines imply that the magic revelation a woman receives when she confronts herself is that she is a sacrificial victim to male sexual desire.

Similarly, in 'Ode for Ted', the man is endowed with enormous creative and controlling powers,

For his least look, scant acres yield.

The poet is not herself but a feminine archetype. She is not even named as Eve, but as "this adam's woman" because of the total power this man exudes:

when all earth his words do summon
leaps to laud such man's blood.

The use of the phrase "this adam's woman" suggests that this ecstasy is universal to all women, and both poems graphically suggest:

Woman wailing for her demon lover.
Kubla Khan, Coleridge.

The sacrificial metaphor of eating and being eaten found in 'Pursuit' is also present in 'The Glutton'. The man is "hunger-strung, hard to slake" while the woman, even more explicitly than in the previous poems, feels:

That all merit's in being meat
Seasoned how he'd most approve.

In 'The Queen's Complaint', a female ruler is reduced to a wanderer after she has sexual contact with a sadistic giant. The giant kills everything that has been most dear to her and yet after he has "solaced her but quit her at cock's crowing", she becomes obsessed by him. She spends her time lamenting his loss and despising her peaceable people:

How sad, alas, it is
To see my people shrunk so small, so small.

All of these poems are archetypally feminine in the way in which they present images of women as willing to the point of masochism to submit to Nietzschean supermen.

Plath continues this image of man as both god and beast in her first collection of poems, *The Colossus*. In the title poem, she uses classical legend and mythology to reconstruct the memory and image of her dead father. The persona of the poem is cast into the ancient role of the female who mourns the dying god and sacrifices to the idol.

The Colossus is the marvellous statue, a figure from mythology, a god, and her father but the Colossus is also bestial for :

> Mule-bray, pig grunt and bawdy cackles
> Proceed from your great lips.

Nothing of value comes from this man cast into a god-like form and yet the woman's life work seems to be spent in serving him:

> Thirty years now I have laboured
> To dredge the silt from your throat
> I am none the wiser.

Just as the woman served her lover's lusts in the previous poems discussed, so she serves at the altar of a dominant male myth in *Colossus*.

Within the last poem of this collection, 'Poem for a Birthday', Plath's attitude towards men begins to change. The poem was written during her first pregnancy which, according to Ted Hughes, was a time when she "changed at great speed".[1] He also speaks of her "receiving herself"[2] at this time. It is a review of her life to date and an attempt to come to maturity before she becomes a mother. Part of this process seems to be asserting a new identity against the claims of her parents.

The father in this poem provides security but he has almost lost his god-like status:

> Once I was ordinary
> Sat by my father's bean tree
> Eating the fingers of wisdom.

Indeed he has "shrunk to a doll". Father and husband become the composite figure of 'The Beast'. The father is the source of all power in childhood and in comparison to the poet's present, 'fusty' state he seems to hold the key to joyous fertility:

> Breathing was easy in his easy holding
> The sun sat in his armpit
> Nothing went mouldy.

However, in order to find herself, Plath must reject him:

> A dustbin's enough for him
> The dark's his bone.

At this point, the father merges inextricably with the husband whose love is seen as animalistic and pathetic:

> He won't be got rid of,
> Mumblepaws, teary and sorry
> Fido Littlesoul, the bowel's familiar.

This dismissal of the husband as a "cupboard of rubbish" obviously links him with the father who similarly "won't be got rid of". Plath seems to realise that her entanglement with the myth of her father and the relationship with her husband will ultimately degrade her:

> I bed in a fishpuddle
> Down   here   the   sky   is   always   falling
> Hogswallow's at the window.

The constant repetition of animal imagery in these early poems suggest that Plath regards men as in some way sub-human, and yet we are also given the image of men as gods. In the whole of her work, there are few poems which deal with men as individuals. Those which do exist are found in the 'middle period' of her poetry in the collections *Crossing the Water* and *Winter Trees*.

The poems, 'Surgeon at 2 am', 'On Deck', 'Zookeeper's Wife', 'Gigolo' and 'Rabbit Catcher' form a series of increasingly bitter portraits of men at work, both in their occupations and in their relationships to the world.

The 'Surgeon at 2 am' represents the musings of a doctor as he performs an operation. His surroundings are lifeless, and he is a depersonalised man who projects anonymity into his surroundings. He forgets that he is operating on another human being:

> As usual there is no face. A lump of
> Chinese white
> With seven holes thumbed in.

He is also totally separate from any spiritual dimension:

> The soul is another light
> I have not seen it.

He is threatened by the beauty of the human body and seems to sense it as a jungle to be tamed and controlled:

> These orchids are splendid. They spot
> and coil like snakes.
> The heart is a red bell bloom, in distress,
> I am so small
> In comparison to these organs!
> I worm and hack in a purple wilderness.

In this poem, the surgeon reduces human flesh to a 'pathological salami' which he regards as something far less efficient and desirable th   "clean, pink plastic limb".

At the end of the operation, the patient is a 'statue' that he has 'perfected' from the anarchic 'purple wilderness' which was the body. He perceives himself as a god, but in reality he is not even human, let alone godlike.

He is as impersonal and emotionally flat as the jeweller in the final stanza of 'On Deck' who is

> Carving
> A perfectly faceted wife to wait
> On him hand and foot, quiet as a diamond.

The persona of 'Zookeeper's Wife' is a sensitive soul lost within the husband's world of hairy, obscene monsters where the beasts and the man seem inseparable. He too is as heartless as the surgeon and the jeweller courting the woman by taking her:

> to play
> With the boa constrictor in the Fellow's Garden.

The snake seems here to be symbolic of the crushing male phallic principle and a destructive element pervades the whole poem. By her immersion in this violent male environment the woman has been made

> lungless
> And ugly.

Unlike the zookeeper, the 'Gigolo' is repellent not for his sweat and animalism, but for his clean efficiency and glitter. He too shares the ability of men to depersonalise others with his way of:

> turning
> Bitches to ripples of silver.

Here is yet another example of a man who in seeing women as mere instruments has also reduced himself to one:

Pocket watch,
I tick well.

The 'Rabbitcatcher' performs the role of the male who snares his prey in a world which is a 'place of force'. Like the rabbits, women are caught to attend the brute violence, and like hunters, men have minds:

like a ring
Sliding shut on some quick thing.

The rabbit appears to have been chosen not only for its fecundity but also for its connotations of the sub-human instinct. Plath concludes that such constriction by a man kills her as surely as he kills the rabbits.

From these individual portraits, Plath moves on in the verse drama, 'Three Women' and in the poems of *Ariel* to make statements about men which have distinctly feminist implications. Men are now seen as a direct threat to the individuality, creativity and sanity of women and the former intense longing for their approval found in the earlier poetry has been replaced by loathing.

The animal images disappear and the female personae of the later work make direct challenges to male power. Beast imagery in relation to men always has sexual connotations in Plath's work and its absence from the later poetry suggests that she is seeking to overcome their power through a transcendence of sexuality. The necessity she seems to see for this transcendence is almost prophetic of the contemporary radical feminist belief that to overcome patriarchy women must end all sexual contact with men.[3]

'Three Women' is a radio verse drama about the reaction to and outcome of three pregnancies. One woman, named the Secretary, miscarries a wanted pregnancy, another named the Wife gives birth to a wanted child and another named the Girl gives up an unwanted child for adoption. The men in this drama are 'jealous gods' of rationality who seem part of an almost cosmic conspiracy directed against women:

> I see the Father conversing with the son
> Such flatness cannot but be holy.
> 'Let us make a heaven,' they say,
> 'Let us flatten and launder the grossness
> from these souls.'

The fertility of women is directly opposed to the rationality of men. Women possess a 'bigness' which 'frightened the mind' of the men from whose 'flatness' the horrors of modern civilisation:

> Bulldozers, guillotines, white chambers
> of shrieks proceed.

The infertility of the Secretary seems to stem from her close association with a male-defined working environment. Plath suggests that this environment is inimical to female creativity:

> When I first saw it, the small red seep,
> I did not believe it
> I watched the men walk about me in the office
> They were so flat
> There was something about them like cardboard
> and now I had caught it.

Similarly, the unwilling motherhood of the Girl is seen as the result of the destructive, flat, male domain whose powers of rationality subjugate women:

> The doctors move among us as if our bigness
> Frightened the mind. They smile like fools
> They are to blame for what I am and they know it.
> They hug their flatness like a kind of health.

The men of *Ariel* have totally lost their status as gods and are now fully cast into the image of fascists and torturers, 'boors' who must be challenged and destroyed. Contemporary feminists have drawn parallels between war, violence, extreme right-wing ideologies and traditional male behaviour. The references to fascism found in 'Daddy' and 'Lady Lazarus' show Plath comparing the arch-masculinity of fascism with the everyday masculinity of the father and husband to whose myths and power she has been subjected. The masculinity which produced the concentration camps is directly related to masculinity in its domestic form where the daughter "never could speak" to, and felt fear of, the father, and where the woman is parasitically drained by the husband:

> The vampire who said he was you
> And drank my blood.

'Daddy' is perhaps Plath's most famous poem. The critic George Steiner has called it "the Guernica of modern poetry." [4] The violence of its imagery and tone with the references to concentration camps, torture, fascism and vampirism certainly evoke the horror of Picasso's most celebrated painting.

Plath claimed that she was adopting the persona of a girl with an Electra complex whose father was a fascist, but while the poem is not completely autobiographical it contains several obvious references to her own life. For example, here she refers to the picture of her father:

> You stand at the blackboard, daddy,
> In the picture I have of you

This is obviously a direct image of the actual photograph the Plaths possessed of Otto in front of his blackboard at the University. Similarly, the "man in black with a Meinkampf look" and the 'vampire' who "drank my blood" for "seven years" is an obvious reference to her perception of Ted Hughes: they had been married for seven years when they separated. But the poem is not completely autobiographical. Otto Plath had no connections whatsoever with Nazism so the poet is moving between the persona's and her own life.

The father who was tended as an idol in 'The Colossus' and the husband or lover to whom submission was ecstasy are metaphorically killed in 'Daddy'. Plath no longer seems possessed by the desperate need for security and protection which permeated the first poem. A comparison of the poems' endings illustrate this point. 'Colossus' ends on a note of empty despair, and we have the sense of the persona standing bereft and helpless before the memory of the dead:

> My hours are married to a shadow
> No longer do I listen for the scrape of a keel
> On the blank stones of the landing.

In 'Daddy', however, we have the sense of the persona in a triumphant, almost exalted state. This is reflected in the language which is no longer the traditional, restrained, poetic diction of the earlier poem but unstrained, slangy and free:

Daddy, daddy, you bastard, I'm through.

The woman who in her early work needed to be sexually possessed by a demon lover, now regards sexuality itself as a need to be transcended:

> I am too pure for you or anyone
> Your body
> Hurts me as the world hurts God.
>
> *Fever 103*

At times in *Ariel*, Plath seems to be expressing a loathing of men which verges on misandry. In the bee poems' sequence, for example, the bees have an all-female society which is both productive and ordered. In 'Wintering', she relates this order to the fact that they have eliminated men:

> The bees are all women
> Maids and the long royal lady
> They have got rid of the men,
> The blunt clumsy stumblers, the boors.

This destruction of men has led to the promise of hope for their community:

> The bees are flying.
> They taste the spring.

In the *Ariel* collection, Plath seems to hold all men responsible for the horrors of modern civilisation. It does not seem to matter whether they are conventionally good or evil. One of her last poems, 'Lady Lazarus', ends on the challenge that it is only the reborn female self who will overcome these horrors:

Herr God, Herr Lucifer
Beware
Beware
Out of the ash
I rise with my red hair
And I eat men like air.

Daddy

CHAPTER FIVE

CHILDREN AND
MOTHERHOOD

Throughout her poetry, Plath seems as ambivalent about motherhood and children as she is about men. She possesses an ultra-feminine stress on the experience of motherhood for, without it, life is considered narcissistic and arid:

> The womb
> Rattles its pod, the moon
> Discharges itself from the tree
> with nowhere to go
> > *Childless Woman*

Moreover, sterility is related very closely to death. Plath uses her usual death symbols when she compares the ovum to the moon and more specifically by referring to the woman's body itself as cadaverous:

> My funeral,
> And this hill and this
> Gleaming with the mouths of corpses.
> > *Childless Woman*

In her earlier poetry, however, she rejects the state of

pregnancy with force and sardonic humour. For example, in 'Metaphors' it is not regarded as any marvel, but as slightly ludicrous:

> I'm a riddle in nine syllables
> An elephant, a ponderous house.

Pregnancy is rejected because the poet feels uninvolved and as if she is an animal,

> I'm a means, a stage, a cow in calf.

The poem's ending does not contain any hope of anticipation but leaves us with a sense of the passivity and unwelcome inevitability of the process:

> I've eaten a bag of green apples
> Boarded the train there's no getting off.

Similarly, in 'Poem for a Birthday', her first directly autobiographical verse, the opening section, 'Who', draws together Plath's pregnancy with her mental hospital experience. The persona is fearful and the pregnancy is not associated with the usual fertility imagery which one would perhaps expect. The creation of new life is taking place in a mouldering, decaying container:

> The month of flowering's finished.....
> This shed's fusty as a mummy's stomach
> Old tools, handles and rusty tusks.

This ambiguous reference to the Egyptian mummy, which encloses a dead body, is also a reference to the womb which contains the unborn child. For Plath, pregnancy seems to be an experience of self-immolation.

This sense of self-sacrifice is comparable to the same loss of self which a mental breakdown also incurs. It also evokes similar emotions. The usual connotations of child-bearing as part of a vegetative life cycle are deliberately reversed, for the persona wishes to "sit in a flowerpot" and prevent life from occurring:

> My heart is a stopped geranium
> If only the wind would leave
> my lungs alone.

In the second section, 'Dark House', the subject is once more returned to pregnancy and the comparison of the womb to a "dark house very big" suggests that she regards childbearing as a conscious attempt to build a security from the depths of the self:

> I made it myself
> Cell by cell from a quiet corner.

This security is itself threatened, for what is contained in the dark house may be even more appalling than present reality:

> Any day I may litter puppies
> Or mother a horse. My belly moves.

Thus any solution found in pregnancy is only temporary, if it exists at all, for the last lines of this section indicate that its acceptance incurs a soft, easy and enervating domestic life:

> It is warm and tolerable
> In the bowel of the root
> Here's a cuddly mother.

In this early work, Plath senses the contradiction between the demands of motherhood and the needs of an intellectual/creative woman which contemporary feminists have described. Like them, she apprehends that there is no easy solution to this conflict. Throughout much of her later work, instead of rejecting motherhood, she is trying to reconcile its demands with the feminist striving to think and create.

The verse drama, 'Three Women', is particularly interesting for the light it throws on Plath's beliefs about children and motherhood. In the drama, she embodies dominant themes in three different aspects of motherhood. The poem seems an attempt to generalise about motherhood as it is not autobiographical, although Plath may well have drawn upon her own experiences of birth and miscarriage. Moreover, the characters are not personally named individuals, but rather representatives of roles for women in society. Plath calls them the Wife, the Secretary and the Girl. Their experiences can then be considered as typical, rather than individual.

The Wife's experience is the pivotal one in the poem for she is completely fulfilled by her pregnancy and is satisfied with the total introspection which it brings:

> I am slow as the world, I am very patient
> Turning through my time, the sun and the stars
> Regarding me with attention.

However, its greatest benefit is that it has removed the necessity for the woman to control her own life. She has achieved a raison d'etre without any conscious mental effort:

> When I walk out, I am a great event,

I do not have to think or even rehearse
What happens in me will happen
                    without attention.

The birth of the child is at first satisfying and
accorded a stereotyped feminine reaction:

What did my fingers do before they held him?
What did my heart do with its love?
..........I shall not let go.

But even though the Wife accepts motherhood she
appreciates its limitations, for the child cannot erase the
inadequacies of his mother or the cruelties of the world:

How long can I be a wall, keeping the wind off?....
Gentling the sun with the shade of my hand
Intercepting the blue bolts of a cold moon?

The woman's acceptance of motherhood is redeeming
in its unalloyed love for her child but it has as a consequence her denial of herself and a desperate refusal to
confront any of the disasters in modern life:

I am simple again I believe in miracles
I do not believe in those terrible children
Who injure my sleep with their white eyes,
their fingerless hands......
I shall meditate upon normality
I shall meditate upon my little son.

The Secretary represents working, thinking,
'masculine' woman and unfulfilled motherhood - a
woman who can only 'make deaths'. Plath suggests that
her inability to have children stems from her close association with the male environment already discussed. Her

infertility comes from her concentration on the world and an inability to be natural:

> I have tried not to think too hard I have tried to
> be natural.
> I have tried to be blind in love, like other
> women.

After her miscarriage, she accepts her fate and identifies herself as sexless and completely subordinated by the world of men:

> I see myself as a shadow, neither
> man nor woman,
> Neither a woman, happy to be like
> a man, nor a man
> Blunt and flat enough to feel no lack.
> I feel a lack...
> I shall be a heroine of the peripheral.

The Girl fulfils the biological requirements of motherhood but is unable to carry out its long term functions. She is almost a complete contrast to the other women in her attitude towards her fate. The Wife's acceptance of consequences and the Secretary's desire that life should be composed of acts which lead to expected results is opposed by the Girl's revulsion against biological progression:

> Every little word hooked to every little
> word, and act to act,
> A hot blue day had budded
> into something.

At birth, there is no miraculous transformation from pain

to love as experienced by the Wife, but a further wish to relinquish her predicament:

I am not ready for anything to happen
I should have murdered this, that murders me.

The Girl is reluctant to admit to any love for her daughter who is regarded as a threat to her identity:

Her cries are hooks that catch and
                    grate like cats
It is by these hooks she climbs
                    to my notice.

She decides to give her baby up in order to return to university. Like the Secretary, however, she has lost a dimension. Plath appreciates the antipathy which exists between maternity and social and mental independence for women in her culture. To show that "I am serious" the Girl must reject her child:

I leave someone
Who would adhere to me
I undo her fingers like bandages
I go.

In this poem, Plath provides a vivid, feministic illustration of the fact that there is no satisfactory fulfilment of motherhood in our culture. The Wife is fulfilled biologically, emotionally and socially but at the expense of her ability to think. The Secretary thinks too much and can only "create corpses" while the Girl, in order to retain her intellect, must repudiate her child.

While Plath is aware of the barriers which motherhood presents to the creative woman, children as individuals are presented in a very positive light: at times as the only salvation for the tortured self. The child poems in the collection, *Winter Trees* and *Ariel* are all expressions of tenderness and protectiveness for children, which are opposed to the mother's emotions of isolation and despair:

In the poem, 'Child', for example, the infant's:

> clear eye is the one absolutely beautiful thing

and the mother is imbued with despair at her inability to:

> to fill it with color and ducks.

In fact, she is instead providing her young with images of grief:

> .....this troublous
> Wringing of hands, this dark
> Ceiling without a star.

In 'Nick and the Candlestick', the mother is conscious of the dangers which surround her child, which include her own perceptions:

> Black bat airs
> Wrap me, raggy shawls
> Cold homicides
> They weld to me like plums.

She is also aware of the terrors of the universe and the world:

the stars
Plummet to their dark address
Let the mercuric
Atoms that cripple drip
Into that terrible well.

In his innocence, the child offers redemption for the mother, just as Christ offered salvation for the world. The faith and hope she cannot find in religion is found through her love for her son, who is given the status of Christ in her life:

You are the one
Solid the spaces lean on, envious.
You are the baby in the barn.

While most of the poems about children found in *Ariel* are happy, they are not entirely free from conflict. Children are recognised as potential barriers to creativity:

The blood jet is poetry
There's no stopping it
You hand me two children, two roses.
Kindness

A resolution of this dilemma is formed in 'Morning Song'. The baby is loved and the mother has a physically symbiotic relationship with it:

One cry, and I stumble from bed.

She realises that while it might heighten her perception, the baby is essentially an individual, not a possession nor indeed a total justification for her own existence:

I'm no more your mother
Than the cloud that distils a mirror to
reflect its
own slow
Effacement at the wind's hand.

Children are to be loved and valued, but this poem
seems prompted by the intuition that they provide no
answers to the question of why and how their parents
should live:

Our voices echo magnifying your arrival.
New statue
In a drafty museum, your nakedness
Shadows our safety.
We stand round blankly as walls.

CHAPTER SIX
WOMEN

Plath loathed womanhood,
her own and in general. [1]

It is my tragedy
to have been born a woman. [2]

The sexual oppression of women is recognised in Plath's poetry but there is little empathy or sympathy for other women, much less sisterhood in her work. Women are berated as dumb blonde cardboard figures (see, for example, 'The Applicant'), derided as old maids ('Spinster' and 'Two Sisters of Persephone') or despised for becoming housewives, neurotic 'Sad hags' who "can't communicate" ('Lesbos'). Her conclusion seems to be that it is the fate of all women to be consumed by 'abortions' and 'bitchery' ('Winter Trees') or domestic drudges lacking the powers of perception of the poet:

> Will they hate me
> These women who only scurry
> Whose news is the open cherry, the open clover?
> *Stings*

Such hostility towards other women is obviously not feminist. It is in examining her attitude towards other women that I believe we can find what Plath was trying to do in all her work: re-evaluate herself in a culture which was hostile to female creativity. While the cultural pressures towards wife/mother conformity of the 1950's and early '60's did not prevent Plath from writing, she would have regarded herself as an anomaly amongst women of the time. She described herself as a "rabid teenage pragmatist"[3] and as we have already seen, she seemed to regard her society as unchangeable. She was, therefore, at odds in a highly individual sense with the way in which society defined her as a woman. The hostility towards other women which is present in her work has to be seen in this context.

'Two Sisters of Persephone' is a good example of a poem in which Plath reveals yet again her perceived dichotomy between thinking and fertile woman. The characters of the poem seem to represent the conflict within Plath herself between intellectualism and femininity. The first woman sits in a "dark wainscotted room" preoccupied by sterile calculations which affect her actual body:

> Dry ticks mark time
> As she calculates each sum
> At this barren enterprise
> Rat shrewd go her squint eyes
> Root pale her meager frame

The second character is a Lawrentian archetype, a woman connected to the Earth:

> the second lies...Lulled
> Near a bed of poppies.

As a prize for unthinking sensual abandon the woman "bears a king" while the intellectual dies "worm-husbanded, yet no woman."

In the poem, 'Spinster', Plath continues with this motif of the barrenness of single life for women. The protagonist of the poem, unlike the mathematician of 'Two Sisters of Persephone', is initially open to men. She is walking with "her latest suitor" when she experiences a panic attack brought on by the disorder she perceives around her. The excursion is taking place in Spring and the girl is obviously threatened by the beginnings of new life

> Found herself , of a sudden, intolerably struck
> By the birds' irregular babel
> And the leaves litter.

The creativity of the season is linked to sexual feelings which she feels she must repress because of the disorder they entail:

> By this tumult afflicted, she
> Observed her lover's gestures unbalance the air,
> Her gait stray uneven
> Through a rank wilderness of fern and flower.
> She judged petals in disarray,
> The whole season sloven.

She decides that she prefers winter:

> Scrupulously austere in its order
> Of white and black.

to the madness of 'bedlam spring'. She withdraws to her own house, from men and from life itself:

And round her house she set
Such a barricade of barb and check
Against mutinous weather
As no mere insurgent man could hope to break
With curse, fist, threat
Or love, either.

A sense of being an exception amongst women
pervades Plath's poems about the relationship between
herself and others. She is no social revolutionary and
lacks the consciousness of the fact that society can
change. This is an essential attribute of feminism. In her
own life, Plath was trying to be a successful creative
artist, sexually fulfilled woman *and* a mother. Yet the
society she lived in regarded this attempt as doomed to
failure. Many of her poems seem to reflect her own deep
fears that she was attempting the impossible.

In spite of seeing the condition of women as being
fixed, Plath occasionally does relate it to the society in
which she lived. The poem 'Lesbos', while perhaps the
most blatantly antagonistic towards another woman in the
whole Plath oeuvre, is ultimately one in which Plath
makes strong connections between the individual
experience of oppression and the social pressures which
produce it.

It was apparently inspired by the unsuccessful and
acrimonious visit of a couple whose marriage was in
nearly as desperate a state as Plath's own. Although the
actual visit was to Plath's North Tawton home the poem's
action takes place in the other woman's house. This
demonstrates the fact that Plath did not, as some critics
have asserted, hysterically write confessional slices from
her own life as they arose.

'Lesbos' is almost a paradigm of Wordsworth's dictum

that "all good poetry is the spontaneous overflow of powerful feelings." (Preface to The Lyrical Ballads, 1798) But in common with the early Romantics, Plath was attempting to compose poems which were the products of strong "emotion recollected in tranquillity." (ibid)

Plath constructs an almost cinematic image of the other woman's house and of the two women dissecting their failed relationships as they neurotically try and fail to cook a meal and look after their children. All the worst aspects of being a middle class Western female of the epoch are found in this poem. The families' food is being prepared in an atmosphere of hate and resentment which is vividly evoked in the onomatopoeic opening lines:

> Viciousness in the kitchen
> The potatoes hiss.

The setting is an exclusive female hell racked by the tensions of unrelieved domesticity. Like a prison or torture cell the kitchen is 'windowless'. Just as prisoners and torture victims are often dehumanised, so the poem's protagonists have been reduced by their pain into inhumane behaviour.

The women seem utterly immured in a maelstrom of unrelieved violent passions which threaten actual physical violence, although they never deliver it. They are cruel to the children and animals, the beings a little more inferior to them in the social scale. Far from being a proud, caring and hopeful mother the poem's speaker fantasises that her child is a 'schizophrenic'. Instead of reassuring her friend, the other woman also pours scorn on the distressed child and suggests that she too should be murdered to prevent her future suicide:

You say I should drown the kittens.
Their smell!
You say I should drown my girl.
She'll cut her throat at twenty
    if she's mad at two.

The despair and anger in this poem are a striking contrast to its title 'Lesbos'. Sappho, the greatest poet of the ancient world, lived on the island of Lesbos within a creative, peaceful and matriarchal culture. By the use of this contrast, Plath seems to be indicating that it is the society which has reduced the women in the poem to the appalling condition in which they find themselves.

But even in this bitter verse, the hostility generated seems aimed at the culture which produced this "venomous opposite" rather than the woman herself or women in general. Plath closely associates the despair and neuroticism of the other woman with the society outside the kitchen's hell by referring to the woman's previous life in Hollywood:

Once you were beautiful
In New York, in Hollywood, the men said,
"Through?"
Gee baby, you are rare.

The other woman's malevolent presence is inextricably related to domesticity and her social role. She is trapped in a loveless marriage where she must emotionally nurture an impotent man:

Every day you fill him with soul
stuff like a pitcher.

All women in this condition are subjected to some form of dehumanisation and an inability to relate to each other.

This leads to self-hatred for the poet: "And I love, am a pathological liar." In 'Lesbos', Plath seems not so much to be rejecting the woman as the destructive, parasitical existence which both of them endure.

By the time she wrote the poems in *Ariel*, Plath had begun to develop a distinct, female poetic identity which stressed the unique nature of female experience and out of which she attempted to construct a valid, alternative life. The early ambivalence on the nature of this female identity found in poems such as 'Two Sisters of Persephone' and 'Spinster' has gone. She seems completely assured of her female identity and has moved forward towards self-acceptance. Perhaps this is the reason for the fine poems of maternal love found in *Ariel*.

There is also strong biographical evidence for this assertion. In the period during which she was writing these poems, Alvarez visited her and comments that she was

> No longer quiet and withheld, a housewifely appendage to a powerful husband, she seemed made solid and complete, her own woman again.[4]

When she had achieved this transformation, Plath was able to reject more forcibly and insistently the traditional world of women and conventional female values. The nature of these values and their rejection are clearly illustrated in 'The Applicant', 'Munich Mannequins' and 'Stings'.

The satirical and amused tone of 'The Applicant' establishes Plath's distance from the woman of the poem. Her servicing function in marriage is both ludicrous and frightening for her willingness

> to bring teacups and roll away headaches
> And do whatever you tell it

reduces her to an object. Throughout the poem she is referred to as 'it'. Marriage is clearly seen as an emotional panacea for wider social evils:

> Will you marry it?
> It is waterproof, shatterproof, proof
> Against fire and bombs through the roof.

This disguises reality and offers no alternatives:

> You have a hole it's a poultice
> You have an eye it's an image
> My boy it's your last resort.

'Munich Mannequins' echoes the fear which Plath feels about her society's tendency to reduce women to objects. The mannequins she describes are the epitome of the cultural ideal of female beauty, but it is a beauty which is appallingly artificial and without rational or emotional purpose:

> Naked and bald in their furs,
> Orange lollies on silver sticks
> Intolerable without mind.

This elevation of stereotyped female beauty has, as its consequence, the renunciation of fertility. One gains the impression that it is not just the fertility of children that this form of beauty has sacrificed but also that of art. This perfection leads to the ultimate horror: the entire extinction of identity:

> Voicelessness. The snow has no voice.

The assertion of a new identity is particularly

apparent in 'Stings'. By a complex comparison and identification of herself with the queen bee, Plath demonstrates an allegory of the relationship between herself and other women. The poet searches for the queen bee in the bee box, wonders if she exists and if she is exceptional. The inclusion of herself immediately following this speculation suggests that the queen bee is a symbol of her own search for an individual female identity and strength against the powers of convention:

> Poor and bare and unqueenly and even shameful
> I stand in a column
> Of winged unmiraculous women
> Honey drudgers.

She has discerned her essential difference from these degraded, 'honey drudgers' but has been unable to assert it. She has, therefore sought security in identification with them and their values:

> I am no drudge
> Though for years I have eaten dust
> And dried plates with my dense hair
> And seen my strangeness evaporate
> Blue dew from dangerous skin.

Unlike the "winged unmiraculous women", Plath sees herself as rising above the common female concerns of the women of her generation. She has created for herself the role of the "sweet God" ('The Arrival of the Bee Box') of artistic creation. It is, however, an extremely lonely, isolated predicament, well analysed by Joyce Carol Oates,

> Between the archetypes of jealous, ruthless
> power, represented by the Father/Son of religious

and social tradition, and the archetypes of
moronic fleshly beauty.....
.......there is very small space for the creative
intellect, for the employment and expansion of a
consciousness that tries to transcend such
limits.[5]

CHAPTER SEVEN

BUILDING AN IDENTITY:
MODELS FOR
CULTURAL VICTIMS

*You may not know what I mean by the Angel
in the House.... She was intensely sympathetic. She was immensely charming. She
was utterly unselfish.... She sacrificed
herself daily, she never had a mind or a
wish of her own. And when I came to write
I encountered her with the very first
words.... She slipped behind me and
whispered: "My dear you are a young
woman.... Be sympathetic; be tender; flatter;
deceive; use all the arts and wiles of our sex.
Never let anybody guess that you have a
mind of your own.* [1]

Before Plath was born, Virginia Woolf had drawn
attention to the spectre of ideal femininity which
has perhaps haunted every woman who has ever
put pen to paper. This spectre has almost
certainly been sitting on the shoulder of every woman

writer since the 19th. century. The notion that women are only valuable if they are altruistic to the point of self-abasement is so deeply embedded within Judeo/Christian/Islamic traditions and cultures that it has become as much a definition of womanhood as the possession of a womb. Sacrifice and self-effacement are crucial components of 'normal' female identity. Plath's integration of this concept into her own psyche is well illustrated in the memorable lines:

And I have had no face,
I have wanted to efface myself.

Tulips

The force of this ideal varies from epoch to epoch, but during Plath's formative years it was at one of its zeniths. One way women writers have dealt with the pressure towards female conformity has been by either not marrying or, if married, not having children. Male writers have never faced the conflict between the demands of children and the demands of art. It has been possible for them to enjoy families, homes *and* creativity. This state of affairs has been both expected by them as a right and implicitly sanctioned by their culture.

Plath herself seemed to find marriage no bar to her creativity. But when she had children, the threats to her artistic ambitions seemed to loom very large in her life. Her diaries and letters at this time are crammed with details of her attempts to find domestic help and a constant struggle to juggle writing and housework.

Of course, to some extent, this is a perennial problem for any woman whose mind aspires to larger vistas than those normally experienced by the housewife. But as we have seen, the 1950's were not only fallow in terms of feminist influence but also constricted any form of non-conformity.

In one of the last essays she wrote whilst she was at Smith, Plath complained that the American educational system placed little emphasis on recognising and nurturing individual talent. She went on to write that there was no place in American culture for the artist.[2] Perhaps she was mistaking her culture's hostility towards the woman artist and/or intellectual for general antipathy towards all artists, irrespective of gender. The feting of Dylan Thomas, for example, in the 1950's demonstrates that America was not totally indifferent to the claims of poetry written by men.

The similarity of the experiences of women with those of ethnic minority groups has often been pointed out. Margaret Atwood and Arnold Rampersad have devised descriptive theories of ethnic minority writing which can be usefully applied to women writers.

They write that the first reaction to being a cultural victim is a complete denial of the victimisation and a suppression of the anger it entails. The person who denies their status as victim is usually in a better situation than their fellow victims and is afraid to lose their advantages if they identify with other victims.

The second attitude Rampersad and Atwood describe is one where the victim acknowledges victimisation as existing but regards it as an

> ....act of Fate, the Will of God, the dictates
> of biology (in the case of women for example),
> the necessity decreed by History or
> Economics, of the Unconscious, or any other
> large powerful idea [3]

They state that the person in this position feels self-scorn for themselves and scorn and hatred for their fellow victims. But they also feel a sense of personal worth for which they can find no definition in their culture. They analyse this as a state of 'double consciousness' which the leading black intellectual, W.E.B. Dubois, has described as

> a sense of always looking at oneself through the eyes of others, of measuring one's soul by the tape of a world that looks on in amused contempt and pity. [4]

The third phase in response to victimisation is to respond to it with anger: to refuse to see oneself as a natural or fated victim. At this point, there is a release of the pent-up energies which had been accumulating during the years of refusal of reality or passive acceptance of its inevitability. This anger may be understandable but it can also be violent and destructive if the subject does not enter the fourth state of transcendence.

This fourth condition is what Rampersad describes as the "reintegration of the self." [5] It is also what Atwood calls the stance of the "creative non-victim." [6] Those who are in this state do not identify with the oppressor, or find their identity in the role of victim, or need to use all their energies in casting off the victim role, for it no longer tempts them. They have transcended the anger of position three which can, without this transcendence, easily revert to the fatalistic vision of position two. They have moved forward to a new sense of self and a more fertile basis for creativity.

Gelpi maintains that if this model is applied to American women's poetry, then Plath is one of the writers who is most representative of the position two consciousness of regarding one's fate as predetermined. She sees her as being trapped on a wheel of man-hatred, woman hatred, body and self hatred, although she acknowledges that Plath opened up the poetic possibilities for other women poets to legitimately express their anger.

Gelpi also makes interesting comparisons between Plath and her contemporary, Adrienne Rich, pointing out that Rich is a poet who can be said to have gone through all the positions discussed during her poetic career.

Much of Plath's poetry is indeed the voice of the passive victim who feels herself to be set apart from her fellow sufferers under patriarchy. A good example of this fated, but aware victim position is the poem, 'All the Dead Dears'.

The woman's skeleton, which is the subject of this work, was discovered with the remains of a mouse and a shrew as tomb-mates. One cannot help but compare these companions with the possessions often buried with entombed males. Plath, however, seems to revel in the fact that the body was found being eaten by the more lowly orders of creation. Indeed, she sees it as a subject of comedy. There is a certain lightness of tone in her observations. The woman wears a 'granite grin' and there is little pity for the fate of a human who becomes animal feed:

> These three, unmasked now, bear
> Dry witness
> To the gross eating game
> We'd wink at if we didn't hear
> Stars grinding, crumb by crumb.

She identifies with the woman on the level of victim. Though the corpse is:

                                no kin
                                Of mine

Plath regards her as symbolic of the fate of women, for she
goes on to state "yet kin she is." When the poet looks into
the mirror, she does not see her own reflection, but those
of her female ancestors, perhaps trying to reclaim her for
the traditional concerns of women:

>   Mother, grandmother, great-grandmother
>   Reach hag hands to haul me in,

to witness:

>   wakes, weddings,
>   Childbirths or a family barbecue:

The poem also ends on a note of despair. We leave it with
the feeling that women are condemned to re-enact the
"gross eating game" because of the strength of their
submission in History:

>   All the long gone darlings: they
>   Get back, though soon,.......until we go
>   Each crossboned Gulliver
>   Riddled with ghosts, to lie
>   Deadlocked with them,
>   taking root as cradles rock.

Given that Plath believed that society would not
change in terms of the power relationship between the
sexes, it is easy to understand why Gelpi places her
within this aware victim position. However, she seems to
be underestimating the development in Plath's work,
especially the force of the anger of the later poems and

their assertion of the poet's separation from the Angel in the House stereotype. The comparison with Rich (in Rich's favour) also seems slightly unfair. Rich has outlived Plath. At the time of Plath's death in 1963 they were both writing from the position three consciousness of an angry victim. Indeed Plath was probably giving a wider vent to her anger than Rich, who at this time was still writing in rather restrained language.

There is also, in Plath's later poetry, some movement towards transcendence of this anger. This transcendence is not done in a directly political way. Rampersad and Atwood imply that participating in radical politics is the only method of overcoming rage from a cultural victim position. Plath, however, began a form of transcendence of her identity as victim from a rediscovery of ancient, female, strength which she found within the spiritual tradition of the Great Goddess.

CHAPTER EIGHT

BUILDING IDENTITY: MYTHOLOGY AS POETIC SOLUTION

According to several writers, Western society has been without access to the spiritual, feminine principle for over 2,000 years. This has led to an ascendancy of male values which now threaten life itself. Adam McLean writes:

> The patriarchal religions triumphed outwardly, imposing their will on humanity. This patriarchal period......saw the development of various abilities in the human soul: the mastery of the physical world through imperialism, the development of a material scientific tradition wedded to a technological culture, the exploitation and rape of the limited resources of the Earth, and the organisation of aggression in society through nationalistic wars. [1]

Any culture's religion and mythology offer important archetypes, role models and patterns on which its members base their behaviour and actions. As Caitlin Matthews remarks,

Myth, story and scripture, however, are all forms of texts to live by. [2]

Our Western Judeo/Christian tradition gives us a model of the Universe with a God who is Father, Son and Spirit rolled into one, with woman cast into the role of either temptress or asexual mother.

The Greek and Roman strands of our tradition have slightly more roles open to women, but even they are dominated by the idea of Man as main Creator and Hero (Zeus, his giving birth to Athene, his paramount position amongst the Gods and the the myths of Hercules and Odysseus). Even though women play a far larger part within the Greek and Roman mythologies they are still cast into the role of main trouble bringers into the world (cf the story of Pandora, the Judgment of Paris, Helen and the Trojan War).

There is, however, another spiritual tradition based on the worship of a female deity and female values. Adam McLean sees the Goddess, not as an objective deity (as for example Christians see God), but in a Jungian way, as representative of the forces at work within the human psyche.

This Goddess manifests herself as a triple deity, as Virgin/Maiden, Mother and Crone/Hag. The several Gods of the Romans and Greeks and Yahweh of the monotheistic religions who replaced her cult are mainly Sky Gods. The Triple Goddess is completely of the Earth. Hence her strong connections with agriculture and fertility.

According to McLean and Matthews, the Goddess worked with the Earth and its inhabitants rather than trying to control them with an externally imposed code as the later patriarchal religions have done. The Trinity of the Goddess is far easier to understand than the abstract notion of the Christian trinity. It not only represents the three stages in the fertile woman's life, but also as McLean states:

> ...the complements and opposites of the psyche. Thus she is both gentle and caring and, at the same time, harsh and ruthless. She is full of light and fair visions, but simultaneously can lead one into darkness and terrible horrors. [3]

This is a very different concept to the Judeo-Christian God. This God is celebrated because of his total goodness and unchanging nature. To account for evil, these religions have invented the Devil, a rival subterranean deity who, they believe, enjoys a special relationship with women! For example, in Judaism it is Eve who is first responsible for succumbing to the Devil's temptation when she lets the serpent persuade her to eat the apple. Another instance of this supposed female kinship with Satan can be seen in the 16th. and 17th. centuries when hundreds of thousands of women were burned as witches. This is the spiritual basis of Western society where, at its most extreme, Man equals Light and Good and Woman equals Dark and Evil.

The symbol of the Great Goddess is the Moon. Lunar cycles are particularly important for women who are governed by a biological pattern which, to men, can make them appear irrational and unpredictable. In contrast to Yahweh, the Judeo-Christian God, the Goddess is also cyclic, changeable and challenges linear, patriarchal, one dimensional, abstract thinking.

Male rationalists have often used this cyclical nature of women's lives and experiences as proof of their inferiority. Within the Goddess's spiritual tradition, this cyclicity is not only acknowledged as a fact, but also seen as a positive advantage to women. Cyclicity places them more in harmony with the Earth. Thus, even apparently negative aspects of femininity such as menstruation, can be appropriated as powerful and enhancing. [4] As part of this cyclicity of human life the Goddess religion, like the Eastern religions of Hinduism and Buddhism, incorporates the idea of reincarnation, rather than resurrection, for the afterlife.

Graves asserts that all 'true poetry'[5] illustrates some aspect of the White Goddess and her 'ancient story':

> The central chapters concern the God's losing battle with the God of the Waning Year for love of the capricious and all-powerful Threefold Goddess, their mother, bride and layer-out. The poet identifies himself with the God of the Waxing Year and his Muse with the Goddess; the rival is his blood-brother, his other self, his weird.[6]

The tradition of the Great or Triple Goddess myth offers a powerfully contrasting perspective on the world to that offered in male deity religions. It also affords women a female model which encompasses power, creativity and anger without the sacrifice of their sexuality or motherhood.

Although Plath read Graves's book *The White Goddess* in 1956,[7] it had only a marginal effect on her poetry until around 1961. As her marriage with Ted Hughes became increasingly troubled, Plath began to focus on her own writing and gave less time to him. Judith Kroll comments:

> In an unpublished draft version of her commentary for *Letters Home*, Sylvia Plath's mother expressed the opinion that Plath

was eager always to put her husband's
career ahead of her own as long as she
believed in the solidarity and mutuality of
their marriage; but when it became clear
that her husband was alienated from her,
the long-repressed frustration showed itself
in a fierce and bitter anger. Plath burned
many old manuscripts and concentrated her
energies on her children and writing. [8]

In *The White Goddess* Robert Graves proffers interesting advice to the woman poet. He recognises that she
must be her own Muse for no man can or will perform this
role. He enjoins women to write their own poetry rather
than copying male verse:

However, woman is not a poet: she is either
a Muse or she is nothing. This is not to say a
woman should refrain from writing poems;
only, that she should write as a woman, not
as if she were an honorary man. [9]

He was also aware of the stultification and restrictions
on the female soul which domesticity and marriage
entails. He believed that marriage led to the 'suicide' of
the Muse within women and warned that the "White
Goddess is anti-domestic"; she is the perpetual 'other
woman'.[10] In a private conversation with Judith Kroll,
Ted Hughes remarked that Graves's dictum that "the
Muse must never become a wife" had a very strong
influence on Plath. [11]

Although Plath was possibly not entirely willing and
pleased to be free from the bonds and expectations of her
marriage, one cannot deny that after it ended her poetry
explodes into righteous anger. She stops being a victim

and identifies herself completely with the White Goddess.

She was perhaps too much of a social conformist to embrace political feminism. Also, the contemporary Women's Movement did not emerge until the late sixties and we can only speculate as to what her attitude towards it might have been. It seems more in keeping with her personality that she should have chosen a literary/spiritual method of transcendence.

What is certain is that after she had relinquished the role of wife, she began to follow Graves's advice and wrote as a woman, rather than an 'honorary man'. This can be illustrated by comparisons between her early and late work and will involve further comment on some of the poems already discussed in this book.

Plath's father poems, 'Electra On Azalea Path', 'The Colossus' and 'Daddy' are good examples of her emergence into a new female identity influenced by the Goddess myth. In both 'Electra On Azalea Path' and 'The Colossus', Plath uses classical Greek mythology in a conventional and masculine defined way.

The persona of 'Electra' is a man-identified woman who only values herself through her relationship to a male:

> The day you died I went into the dirt.

As in traditional Judeo-Christian tales, in this poem men are innocent and women guilty of evil. For example, Iphigenia's sacrifice by Agaememnon is portrayed as if he had nothing to do with it directly:

> The day your slack sail drank
> my sister's breath.

Clytemnestra's revenge is referred to as 'evil'. The persona is passive and traditionally feminine:

> Small as a doll in my dress of innocence
> I lay dreaming your epic

She also takes responsibility for the father's death, suggesting that she was born to destroy him:

> The truth is, one late October,
>   at my birth-cry
> A scorpion stung its head,
>   an ill-starred thing;

Female responsibility for the father's death does not stop at the daughter, but goes on to include the mother too:

> My mother dreamed you face down in the sea.

By the time she wrote 'The Colossus', Plath seems to have lost some of the sense of responsibility for her father's fate but, as discussed in Chapter Four, she remains in the classically passive role of the female who mourns the dying god and sacrifices to the idol. She is still prostrating herself on the altar of masculinity and performing a traditionally feminine role.

In 'Daddy', she breaks completely free from the victim position and from the power and influence of men. She appreciates what a victim she has been by referring to herself as a Jew, but transcends this by ceremonially killing her father and husband. This killing is not just an individual one, but is part of a ritual joined in by the whole community:

There's a stake in your fat black heart
And the villagers never liked you.
They are dancing and stamping on you.

Barbara Walker writes that human sacrifice was an important part of ancient Goddess religions:

> Human or animal, the sacrificial victims of ancient cultures were almost invariably male.....Males were expendable, for there were always too many for a proper breeding stock. The same was true of human sacrifices, which were men, not women... Therefore male blood only was poured out on the earliest altars in imitation of the female blood that gave life. [12]

The father figure is also transformed from the God/Hero of the earlier poems into an object. From existing in the daughter's life and imagination as "a bag full of God," he has become a, 'black shoe' and a, 'Ghastly statue' whom she exorcises from her life.

As Judith Kroll points out, rituals of exorcism implicitly entail the idea of rebirth:

> Whenever exorcism, or attempted exorcism, of her father or his proxy occurs it is always as a preliminary to a rebirth which also entails the expulsion of her false self. [13]

This false self can be regarded as the Gravesian rival, blood brother or weird. In Plath's case, the rival is the 'normal woman' or, in literary terms, 'The Angel In The House' of her epoch. As we have seen, some feminists have regarded Plath's hostility towards other women as an indication that she supported traditional femininity. If, however, we read these hostile poems as a dialogue with the rival, or false self within the poet herself, it is possible to place a different perspective on Plath's attitude to other women and femininity.

Four poems written within a month in 1961 (and printed consecutively on pages 157 - 162 in *Collected Poems*) are interesting in this context. The first two, 'Barren Woman' and 'Heavy Women', written on 21st. and 26th February respectively, present two contrasting states of the rival. Whilst Plath seems to have been an enthusiastic mother, she was also aware of the psychic and physical sacrifices that motherhood involves. Through these two poems she conducts a debate between the relative merits of fertility and childlessness.

The barren woman of the first poem is described in the cold and sterile images which Plath usually reserves for men and childless women. Without children the woman is lifeless, a "Museum without statues" haunted by the babies she will never have; "the dead injure me with attentions".

But there remain attractive features about this condition for the woman is still full of a certain classical beauty, "grand with pillars, porticoes, rotundas." Perhaps Plath is not only referring to the womb in these lines but also her own poetry. Like museums with their architecture, her poetry survives, but she does not feel that it has the organic connection with the Earth which bearing children has. The Goddess, in her guise of the Moon, seems to comfort the barren woman, but as Kroll remarks, this signifies not "an alliance with the Moon, but a victimisation by it." [14]

'Heavy Women' are fertile but their fertility also does not gain Plath's approval. They exist in a 'smug' vegetative state and seem, like 'The Munich Mannequins', "without mind":

> they meditate
> Devoutly as the Dutch bulb

These women are not fertile in a creative, but in a passive way. Plath associates them with the male-defined figure of the asexual Virgin Mary when she describes the way the "dusk hoods them in Mary blue". The only possibility of thought comes from men but this is presented in sterile terms for the 'wise men' are 'gray' and will come on "the axle of winter". Their children do not offer any hope, for they are unremarkable figures rather than Messiahs:

> Pink-buttocked infants attend them.
> Looping wool, doing nothing in particular.

Plath alerts the reader to the fact that she is speaking about a universal condition, for all the characters within this poem "step among the archetypes."

The rival, or the other, in these two poems represent the war within the consciousness of the poet between fertility without thought and merely sterile beauty. The next poem was written three weeks later and moves the argument into the poet herself. Ostensibly addressed to a plaster cast on a body, as we read this poem we rapidly forget that the poet's subject is a plaster cast and start to view it as an actual person. Throughout, Plath refers to 'she' and 'me' and it becomes apparent that she is using the cast as an allegorical device for dealing with the rival within herself.

This poem deals with the public persona of Sylvia Plath described by Alvarez as:

> briskly American: bright, clean, competent, like
> a young woman in a cookery advertisement. [15]

This bright All-American housewife (surely the Transatlantic version of the Angel In The House) is counterposed by the "same, identical woman" ('Lady Lazarus') who wrote *The Bell Jar* and the *Ariel* poems.

'In Plaster' begins with the feeling that the poet's situation is intolerable and insoluble:

> I shall never get out of this!

The plaster cast, or public persona, is superficially superior to the body she encases:

> And the white person is certainly the superior one
> She doesn't need food, she is one of the real saints

In contrast, the real self which exists within the public persona or plaster is most unattractive. She is "old yellow", "ugly and hairy".

The plaster cast is an admirable rival for she is "unbreakable", uncomplaining, calm, tidy, patient and a "true pacifist". She possesses all the characteristics of the Angel In The House and is a seductive example to the angry, ugly self she surrounds:

> She humored my weakness like
> the best of nurses.

But like the altruistic, self-effacing woman the plaster symbolises she is without the consciousness which illuminates being. "She had no personality"; she resembles a "dead body". The real self is preferable to this plaster saint because she is capable of endowing her with a sentient life:

Without me, she wouldn't exist.....
I gave her a soul.

The whole poem is a description of Plath's battle with this rival and one feels in it the battle she experienced between the "slave mentality" of the Angel In The House and the vengeful soul trying to hack her way out of the cast. The true self is not as well formed as her rival. She is a, 'half-corpse' but she is determined to break free of her influence and the poem ends on a hopeful note:

> I'm collecting my strength; one day I shall
> manage without her,
> And she'll perish with emptiness then,
>   and begin to miss me.

On the same day as she wrote 'In Plaster', Plath also wrote 'Tulips' which can be read as an attempt by the poet to discover how she can shed the dependence on the plaster-saint public self. In this poem, the persona has entered into a transcendent state which seems akin to the states of consciousness attained by Buddhist meditation:

> I am learning peacefulness,
>   lying by myself quietly
> As the light lies on these white walls,
>   this bed, these hands.
> I am nobody; I have nothing
>   to do with explosions.

She has separated her soul from her body to the point where the body is totally unimportant:

> My body is a pebble.

This has been achieved by a complete renunciation of domesticity and the claims of traditional femininity:

> They have swabbed me clear of my
>   loving associations..........
> I watched my tea set,
>   my bureaus of linen, my books
> Sink out of sight, and the water
>   went over my head.
> I am a nun now,
>   I have never been so pure.

She has obviously been reborn and seems to have incorporated Graves's notion that the White Goddess is anti-domestic. The description of herself as a 'nun' also suggests the incarnation of the Goddess in her Maiden form.

This renunciation is a positive, rather than a deprived experience:

> How free it is, you have no idea how free—
> The peacefulness is so big it dazes you.

It is a state women can rarely attain and the tulips' intrusion is an unwelcome return of those responsibilities which the poet has renounced. They are compared to an 'awful baby' which potentially threatens her existence:

> The vivid tulips eat my oxygen.

While the speaker is literally brought down to earth by the claims which the tulips represent, her perceptions are irrevocably altered for these earthly claims are now associated with "a country far away as health."

Plath's spiritual identification with the Goddess myth

and its stress on the cyclicity rather than the stasis of human existence is apparent throughout the poems written in 1961 and 1962.

In 'The Moon and the Yew Tree', Plath compares the spiritual values of the Goddess with those of Christianity. According to Graves, the yew tree is

> the death-tree in all European countries, sacred to Hecate in Greece and Italy.
> .....The yew is mentioned by Pausanias as the tree beside which Epaminondas found the bronze urn on Mount Uthome, containing on a tin scroll the secret mysteries of the Great Goddess.....
> .....In Brittany it is said that churchyard yews will spread a root to the mouth of each corpse. [16]

Hecate is the aspect of the Triple Goddess who represents the Crone, age and death. Although she is frightening and changeable:

> White as a knuckle and terribly upset.
> It drags the sea after it like a dark crime;
> it is quiet with the O-gape of complete despair.

The poet identifies with Hecate because she presents an image of strength:

> The moon is my mother.
> She is not sweet like Mary.

The Christian religion clearly still holds attractions for the poet: "How I would like to believe in tenderness". However, in imagistic terms, Christianity is forcefully rejected. All the Christian images in this poem are associated with darkness, damp and boredom whilst the images of the Goddess are invigorating and inspiring. For example, the bells which affirm Resurrection are described as sober, the Virgin Mary is a mere 'effigy' while the Christian saints look down on 'cold pews' and have "hands and faces stiff with holiness." For all the terror which Hecate can evoke, she is far more exciting and powerful than the Christian Virgin:

> Her blue garments unloose
> small bats and owls

and "she is bald and wild." As a deity who is in harmony with, rather than above, Nature, she also offers Plath tremendous creative powers, for under her influence

> the grasses unload their griefs on my feet as if I
> were God,

The Goddess tradition involves a belief in continuous rebirth or reincarnation. Barbara Walker writes:

> Literally, 'refleshing' the basic Oriental view of cyclic rebirth after each death; the original meaning of being born again. In the role of Fate-Goddess, the Great Mother governed the Wheel of Becoming (Greek, kyklos geneseon) which meant the cycles of successive lives, like the wheel of karma governed by Kali. Patriarchal thinkers tended to deny the doctrine of reincarnation in favor of the one way trip to heaven or hell after only one life on earth. They sought eternal stasis rather than cycles. [17]

This stress on the importance of rebirth is obviously important in Plath's poetry. 'Lady Lazarus' dices with death in ten year cycles and triumphantly returns with greater strength. Degraded by "the big strip tease" she even makes an art out of dying and returns to confront and destroy her enemies:

> Out of the ash
> I rise with my red hair
> And I eat men like air.

In her Babylonian incarnation as Ishtar, the Goddess had red hair[18] and Plath seems to be threatening her male enemies with the sacrificial death of Ishtar's consort Tammuz.

Plath's last poem, 'Edge', can also be seen within a Goddess inspired reincarnation framework. Plath was familiar with Zen-Buddhism [19] whose followers believe, as did Goddess worshippers, that there is eventually an end to the cycles of death and rebirth and release from the world of suffering. Perhaps this "woman is perfected" because she is on the 'edge' of achieving release from the Wheel of Fate?

She has certainly resolved all the contradictions of her present life. She has reabsorbed her children back into her body where they were once pure and uncorrupted:

> She has folded
> Them back into her body as petals

She is completely contented:

> Her dead
> Body wears the smile of accomplishment.

All the action takes place under the eye of the Goddess who observes the particular action as merely a small part of a universal story:

> The moon has nothing to be sad about,
> Staring from her hood of bone.
> She is used to this sort of thing.
> Her blacks cackle and drag.

CHAPTER NINE
AFTERLIFE

...the loss of it, the terrible loss
of the more she could have done!

Anne Sexton, letter,
20th January 1967 [1]

Everyone has a skeleton in their closet.
But the person who kills themselves
leaves their skeleton in another's closet.

Father of a boy who'd
committed suicide.[2]

The shocking manner of Plath's death at the apparent height of her poetic powers, has meant that her posthumous life has been even more controversial and interesting, to the point of notoriety, than her life itself was.

As we have seen, during their marriage Sylvia was very much in Hughes' poetic shadow. He had won major awards and was receiving great critical acclaim. Reviews of *The Colossus* had not been particularly encouraging and overall, in her literary life, there'd been more rejections than acceptances.

A poignant example of Plath's position is recounted by

Al Alvarez, the poetry critic of *The Observer*. He made a visit to the Hughes family to interview Ted. Towards the end of the visit, Sylvia had commented that she'd been pleased he'd "picked that poem." [3]

Alvarez spent several embarrassed seconds wondering what she was talking about. Sylvia, noticing his blank look, had to remind him that in the previous year he'd published her poem, "Night Shift" in *The Observer*. He then realised that she was not just "a bright young housewife"[4] but Sylvia Plath, the gifted poet. Incidents such as these must have provided her with a regular reminder of her relative lack of success in comparison to Hughes. As Ronald Hayman perceptively comments:

> When Sylvia Plath died, she wasn't yet Sylvia
> Plath: the name had none of the reverberations
> it has today. [5]

Just before she died she appears to have been in financial difficulties, although this has been disputed by the Hughes family.[6] Indeed, her friends' housekeeper, Phyllis, was so disturbed by Sylvia's plight that she gave her some money.[7]

In her last weeks, Sylvia spent a great deal of time in the Becker household. Jillian and Gerry, who lectured in English Literature at Hendon Polytechnic, had met her through their mutual friendship with Helder Macedo, a Portugese poet in exile. This couple gave her much-needed support and appear to have been invaluable friends.

However, the time she spent at their home must also have proved emotionally painful. The Beckers had children and were a dual-career household. They were therefore unwittingly providing her with recurring reminders of her 'failed' marriage.

We must also remember the fact that single parenthood, especially by divorce or separation, was by no means the common experience it is today. Sylvia knew no-one who was in a similar situation to her own. Indeed, it must have felt at times as if she was surrounded by a circle of apparently happily married friends. She was sadly lacking in the type of emotional support which can only come from a confidante who has been in a comparable position.

At a party she was introduced to the novelist Doris Lessing, who might have proved such a confidante and friend. However, Lessing felt that she could not cope with someone whose very presence seemed like a "total demand".[8] Plath died feeling isolated, bereft of the major love of her life and only half-recognised for her abilities as a writer.

We will never know what Plath's reputation would have been if she had not died so early and in such tragic circumstances. There is always a lingering suspicion that the critics who began their paens of praise for her work so soon after her death, might have carried on ignoring it for years if she had gone on living.

The Romantic notion of the doomed artist sacrificing him/herself in the cause of Art is a recurrent theme in Western culture. This aspect of Plath's work was eagerly seized upon immediately after her death. In a memorial talk which was broadcast on Radio Three soon after Plath's death, Alvarez stated:

> The achievement of her final style is to make poetry and death inseparable. The one could not exist without the other. And this is right........ It needed not only great intelligence

and insight to handle the material of them, it also took a kind of bravery. Poetry of this order is a murderous art.[9]

This unfortunate comment is typical of a whole strand of Plath criticism which glamourises her suicide.It is as if her status as an artist depended upon her killing herself. The majority of contemporary critics have regarded Plath as a great poet. In 1982, *The Collected Poems of Sylvia Plath* was awarded the prestigious Pulitzer Prize for poetry. Her greatness is not, however, universally acknowledged. Irving Howe has written that in future years she will be treated as a minor poet of only specialised interest.[10] David Holbrook believes that her work is merely the product of a schizophrenic derangement. He even goes so far as to suggest that it should never be read by young people, for fear of the damaging effect it could have upon their minds.

The emergence of the Women's Movement within a few years of her death also fuelled interest in her life and work. Plath has become almost a paradigm of an intelligent, creative *mother's* experience of the literary/artistic world. Some feminists have even gone so far as to blame Ted Hughes for his wife's death as if he had personally held her head in the gas oven himself. [11]

As several writers have pointed out, Plath's work might well have been written posthumously and in the past thirty years there have been many opportunities for:

> The pea-nut crunching crowd
> Shove in to see
> Them unwrap me hand and foot -
> The big strip tease.

Plath is that rare breed, an acclaimed woman poet. She is, moreover, one who gained fame at an opportune historical moment. Many of the concerns of her life and work also became the preoccupations of a whole generation of women who followed her.

It is not only feminism that has provoked this great interest but also the sense of mystery surrounding her life and work. When we read her poems, for example, just as we feel we have discovered the 'real' Sylvia, up pops another poem or interpretation to confound the search. Similarly in her life, there seem to have been almost as many Sylvia Plaths as there are people who have known and written about her.

Ted Hughes has compounded this mystery by his behaviour and writings about Sylvia in the years following her death. One of the earliest of these strange occurrences was in his choice of the burial place for Plath's body.

An American, living in London and recently moved from Devon, has her final resting place in Heptonstall cemetery, near Hebden Bridge, West Yorkshire. Although Hughes's family lived in Heptonstall, it was a place she had only visited on a few occasions. It was also a relatively inaccessible spot to visit for her young children, close friends, immediate family or admirers. Financial considerations probably prevented the shipping of her body to the States. But from the perspective of her own emotional connections, London or the graveyard adjoining her Devon home, seem more appropriate places for her to be buried. She had herself believed that eventually she would be buried in the North Tawton churchyard. [11]

The other mysteries concern Hughes and his subsequent handling of Plath's work. His dealings with prospective biographers, critics and scholars are also worthy of comment. When Plath died she had not made a will. As she was still married to Hughes, her estate passed to him and he therefore owns all the copyright to her work.

In her flat at 23, Fitzroy Road, he found a huge amount of material which included her manuscript for *Ariel*, detailed and extensive journals, an almost completed novel entitled *Double Exposure*, (which Sylvia thought was better than *The Bell Jar*),[12] a substantial fragment of another novel, short stories and numerous poems. He had not read most of this material, even though the bulk of it had been composed in Devon.[13]

What followed is, from a literary/historical viewpoint, almost unforgivable. Hughes destroyed one volume of her journals because he didn't want Frieda and Nicholas to read them in the future.[14] He has also said that "in those days I regarded forgetfulness as an essential part of survival."[15] He refers to another journal, the novel fragment and the manuscript of *Double Exposure* as having 'disappeared'.[16] Judith Kroll, who saw an outline of *Double Exposure*, has described its plot.[17] From this description, the story sounds as similar to the marital difficulties of Plath and Hughes as *The Bell Jar* was to Sylvia's 1953 breakdown.

Hughes also admits to not publishing Plath's remaining journals in full because he wishes to protect the people about whom she wrote. He has written that he is not sure that she herself would have wanted what were, perhaps, private jottings published because the:

> vivid cruel words she could use to pin down her acquaintances and even her close friends.... would be no joke to the recipients, still less so

now that she is internationally famous and admired for her gift of phrase. [18]

It is easy to be critical of Hughes's actions because they hint so strongly of self-protection. But no-one seems to have seen his behaviour in the light of the trauma endured by the survivors of a suicidal act.[19]

Though Hughes and Plath were separated at the time of her death, there is some doubt that this separation was going to be permanent. The happy and loving years which they had shared together would not have been simply erased by the five months of living apart. Indeed, immediately after Plath was buried, Hughes said to Jillian Becker, a close friend of Sylvia's that "something of me has died with her." [20]

The suicide of a parent is a particularly traumatic event in the life of a child. One adult survivor has described the suicide of his father as his "own personal holocaust".[21] Frieda and Nicholas had lost their mother in the worst way possible. In these circumstances, Hughes's most overriding concern must have been for their future welfare; especially their psychological well-being. It may well have been in their interest to protect them from reading the journal. Plath chronicled her life and emotions in minute detail. She may have been suffering from post-natal depression. The destroyed journal may have contained accounts of frustration and anger directed against the children. It might have provoked needless guilt in them if they had read it in future years.

In the wake of a suicide, close relatives and friends of the perpetrator often take irrational decisions and do seemingly inexplicable things.[22] Anger is a common emotional response. Hughes's destruction of the journal may well have been an act of uncontrollable rage.

Hughes's acquaintance with great tragedy did not end with Plath's death. He maintained a rather volatile stop/start relationship with Assia Wevill. In 1967, she gave birth to their daughter, Shura.

Assia was apparently haunted by Sylvia's fate. She was ostracised by mutual friends and the London literati who held her responsible for the early loss of a genius. In 1969, she imitated Sylvia, gassing both herself and her child.

Hughes's sorrow about Plath's suicide must have been doubly compounded by the loss of his second life partner and his small daughter. This has perhaps been yet another factor in his subsequent behaviour. It is also a reminder of however much we may feel sympathy for the plight of someone who takes their own life, we must not forget the terrible turmoil they leave behind them.

What is less excusable is the way in which Hughes has handled the rest of Plath's work and the way he has treated many of writers and scholars who have written about her.

The *Collected Poems* was not published until 1981, eighteen years after Plath's death. This was an inordinate delay which hampered scholarly work for many years.

He did not publish the *Ariel* collection in the form in which Plath had arranged it. He left out fourteen of the forty-one poems she'd included and added thirteen others which Plath had not intended for publication in the volume. He released these poems amongst others in 1966 and 1971 when he published collections *he'd* arranged and entitled them *Crossing The Water* and *Winter Trees*. This proved very confusing for writers on Plath.

According to Marjorie Perloff, Hughes's rearrangements of, and omissions from, the *Ariel* collection changed the whole structure of the book.[23] She maintains that

Hughes's *Ariel* leads the reader towards the conclusion that Plath was suffering from an inevitable death-wish. Plath's *Ariel* would have been a far more optimistic book. For example, the first poem 'Morning Song' begins with the word 'Love' and the last poem of the collection, which would have been 'Wintering', ended on the note of the bees tasting 'The Spring'.

Biographers and others who have either written or wanted to write about Plath's life have faced serious difficulties in dealing with Hughes. One of the first to do so was Al Alvarez, who was a close friend of the couple. Indeed, he was so close to Hughes that he went with him to the undertaker's to arrange the funeral. He also saw her body.

Eight years after these events, Alvarez wrote *The Savage God,* his study of suicide. Its prologue was a fascinating and perceptive biographical account of Plath in the weeks leading to her suicide. In no way can it be construed as damaging to either poet's reputation.

This prologue was first published in *The Observer* who intended to run it in two parts. After the first part appeared, Hughes obtained an injunction to prevent the second part being published. He claimed that it was not an accurate account of what had actually happened.[24] Hughes went on to attempt to stop the piece being used in the book itself, but did not succeed.[25]

This was just the first in a long series of obstacles which Hughes has since placed in the paths of those who have tried to write about Plath's life or publish her letters.

In 1968, Harper and Row, who were Plath's American publishers, commissioned Lois Ames to write a biography of the poet. Ames interviewed Aurelia Plath, friends and former boyfriends but Hughes, as has always been his practice, did not grant her an interview. Indeed, he even contacted people he knew would be approached for their stories and advised them not to talk with Ames. Eventually, the lack of assistance from the Plath estate in terms of information and permission to quote from the work led to Ames giving up her project in 1975/6.

When feminist interest in Plath's work began in the early 1970's, two other women, Harriet Rosenstein and Elizabeth Hinchliffe started work on biographies which were also commissioned by publishers. Once more, antipathy from Hughes led to nothing being produced, even though both writers did substantial research and all but completed their manuscripts.

Rosenstein had been given her commission on the basis of a dissertation which she had written for Brandeis University. Ted had appointed his sister Olwyn as the agent for Sylvia's estate. According to Paul Alexander, yet another writer who has been hindered by Hughes, Olwyn demanded that Rosenstein's dissertation should be locked away in a safe at Brandeis![26] Rosenstein was so distressed by these events and her contact with the Hugheses that she never wrote about Plath again. In a letter to a friend she wrote, "I don't ever want to be connected with Sylvia Plath."[27]

Edward Butscher, another prospective biographer, also became fascinated by Plath's life and work in the early 1970's. He, however was deflected from the work by Olwyn Hughes who claimed that a "previous contract with Lois Ames" meant that she and her brother could not help him with biographical details.[28] Butscher has recorded how he was "downcast by the realization that important sources of information were cut off from me"[29] Yet at this point, (1973) Ames was facing similar difficulties with the Hugheses!

Butscher went on to edit a book of readings on Plath,

in which he provided an introductory biographical chapter. There is an interesting and cryptic publisher's note accompanying this chapter which states:

> Mr. Butscher wishes to make it known that changes were made in his Introduction by hands other than his own." [30]

Plath's family and friends were not exempt from Hughes's attempts to control all information about Plath. In the mid-70's, Aurelia Plath was eager to reveal the more cheery and optimistic aspects of Sylvia's personality which came through in her letters to her mother. She decided to publish them, but though she was the owner of the letters, Hughes owned their copyright. Once more he stopped an unexpurgated Plath being read by the public. Aurelia would have liked to publish 700 letters but only 384 appeared and even then they had undergone internal cuts. [31]

For several years Gordon Lamayer, Sylvia's last serious boyfriend before Hughes, attempted to publish her letters to him. Obviously, he found a publisher for the work but could not gain Hughes's permission to quote. He was still trying to publish his book when he died in 1991.[32]

It was fully twenty five years after Plath's death that a book length biography finally appeared. In 1988, Linda Wagner-Martin, an American professor of English Literature, produced *Sylvia Plath: A Biography*. When she sent her draft to the Hugheses for permission to quote they specified that she should make cuts of 15,000 words.

Eventually, because she would not change the book as much as Hughes wanted, Professor Wagner-Martin was forced to drastically reduce her quotations from Plath's work to the point where they fell within a 'fair use' interpretation of the copyright laws. The book is now 150 pages shorter than the original manuscript and is not as the author intended it to be. In spite of these substantial cuts, when the publishers began to distribute it, a law suit was threatened.[33] Wagner-Martin is a feminist and it seems as if Hughes's opposition to the book rests on her mode of interpretation, rather than whether it is factually inaccurate or presents him in a bad light.

Hughes also entered into personal vilification of Linda Wagner-Martin. In a letter he wrote to her British publishers, Chatto and Windus, which was subsequently quoted in *The Independent* (12th. March 1988), he stated:

> She's so insensitive that she's evidently escaped the usual effects of undertaking this particular job - ie mental breakdown, neurotic collapse, domestic catastrophe - which in the past has saved us from several travesties of this kind being completed.

This almost reads as if Plath exerts malevolent powers from her grave which are equivalent to the Curse of Tutankhamun! It is more likely that any misfortunes which befell previous writers who tried to publish biographies on Plath were the results of negotiating with the Hugheses.

Since Wagner-Martin's work was published, three other writers have been embroiled in battles with the Plath estate. The biographer Ronald Hayman could not obtain permission to quote directly from Plath's poetry for his book, *The Death And Life of Sylvia Plath*. He therefore had to paraphrase her lines whenever he discussed the poetry. This is a book which might otherwise have proved a stimulating introduction to the non-specialist reader. It has however, been rendered awkward to read by the restrictions under which Hayman was operating.

An academic, feminist writer Jacqueline Rose, Reader in Literature at the University of Sussex, initially gained permission to quote for her own critical study *The Haunting Of Sylvia Plath*. Hughes later tried to rescind this because of her reading of a particular poem, 'The Rabbit Catcher'. Although its publishers Virago were warned by the Hugheses that the book would not appear, they ignored their objections and went ahead. Rose was so shaken by her correspondence with Hughes that she added a preface to her book which gives an account of it. She writes that her book was called 'evil' by Hughes[34] and more chillingly that he considered that

> speculation of the kind I was engaging in about Sylvia Plath's sexual identity would in some countries be "grounds for homicide" [35]

Paul Alexander, the author of the most recent Sylvia Plath biography, *Rough Magic*, claims that he has written "the longest, most complete version of Plath' s life to date."[36] This book has been given good reviews in the United States. It has not been published in this country because Hughes regards it as defamatory. Britain has more restrictive libel laws than the USA, so it is unlikely that it will ever be made available here.

I have recently obtained a copy of *Rough Magic* from a friend who lives in the USA. It is the fullest and most interesting of all the Plath biographies. While it is certainly controversial, it is a shame that it is never likely to be published in Britain as its contents would provoke a fascinating debate. Anyone who has a serious scholarly interest in Plath should try to read this work.

To anyone seriously interested in Plath, this whole sorry story of abandoned, unpublished and mutilated books is enraging. If it were the State which was exercising this type of censorship and creating this climate of fear around a writer, it would rightly be called totalitarian and dictatorial. Under our present laws, one individual is able to exert what seems like an inordinate degree of control over the writings of a major writer and those who wish to write and read about her. Ultimately, we can only read what Hughes will allow us to read.

One biography has, however, received the Plath estate's seal of approval. *Bitter Fame* by Anne Stevenson is the only biographical study of the poet to gain full permission to quote from the work. Stevenson was also given extensive access to the Hughes' archives. The result has been not so much biography as character assassination.

In this particular book, Plath appears as a selfish, demanding, sexually rapacious and deviant woman permanently living on the borders of psychosis. From her birth in 1932, until her death in 1963, she seems like a person who tortured her own family, the Hughes family and her close friends. Many of Plath's friends have been appalled by Stevenson's version of events. Alvarez refers to this biography as "three hundred and fifty pages of disparagement". [37]

But Stevenson is not in fact the sole author of the book which bears her name. In her Author's Note, she states that "it is almost a work of dual authorship" [38] between herself and Olwyn Hughes. The royalties of the book have been divided in such a way as to make it plain that Olwyn's name should also be on the cover. Olwyn receives 40% of the British and 30% of the American royalties for *Bitter Fame*.

The feminist *issues* about gender and writing which have become so central in the debate on Plath are never mentioned in this work. Feminism and feminists are referred to merely in order to denigrate them. During a study day on Plath held at York in October 1991, Stevenson, a guest speaker, was extremely evasive about her opinions on Plath's relationship to feminism. At times, she also seemed utterly dumbfounded by questions which centred around anecdotes appearing in her book. [39]

As we have seen, Plath was frequently so prescient that we can almost suspect her of clairvoyance. She seemed to have foreknowledge that her life would become such a rich source of interpretation and disputation. For example, in her journal of 1958 she wrote:

> My life, I feel, will not be lived until there are
> books and stories which relive it perpetually
> in time. [40]

This book will surely not be the last attempt to do so.

CONCLUSION

Whilst there are certainly traces of classically feminine characteristics such as submission to men in Plath's early poetry, these had disappeared when she wrote her later work. At this time, it is indeed possible to use the adjective feminist to describe poems such as 'Daddy', 'Lady Lazarus' and the bee sequence.

We cannot, however, describe her as a feminist in the contemporary sense of the word. Above all, feminism implies a notion of *sisterhood* with other women. It also entails a belief in the possibility of social change and usually a commitment to taking action in the feminist cause. Plath saw herself as an exception amongst women, especially those domestically oriented women of the American 1950's. The victim of an identity crisis, she was at odds in a highly individual way with her society's definition of true womanhood.

Much of her poetry is concerned with trying to carve out a measure of self-definition as a woman artist against all those forces trying, within her own mind, to reclaim her for traditional femininity. Thus we find an *intellectual* dissociation from other women at the same time as she identifies herself with the *biological* fate of womanhood.

In the light of the development of the Women's Movement, it has been easy to suppose that Plath was developing into a feminist poet. Although her poetry sometimes feels as if it were written post-1968, her death predates the rise of contemporary feminism. It seems unlikely that she would have identified with the Women's Movement in the wholehearted way that, for example, her contemporary, Adrienne Rich has done.

She did, however, resolve some conflicts within her later poetry. It is interesting that she chose the literary/spiritual model of the White Goddess rather than a socio-political model to do so. While the White Goddess mythology gave her a strong female image with which to identify, it was only too predictable that she should choose that particular framework for her expression of female power. Mythology was a dominant mode of literary criticism in the 1950's. The influence of T.S. Eliot with his emphasis on mythology in poetry was particularly strong. Plath's use of Graves' work seems a quintessentially 1950's choice.

Her conviction that society was unchangeable meant that her newly forged 'Sweet God' identity was one which could only be applied to herself. She also felt compelled to re-enact the mythology of the Goddess and be reborn. To do so she needed to die or undergo a ritual death.

There is evidence that her death was a parasuicide which went wrong[1] and that she intended to symbolically die, presumably to rise at the start of another of her ten year cycles. If Plath took the Goddess religion's belief in reincarnation to its logical conclusion, then her physical death is of little account. She would be reborn into another life or 'perfected' and released from the Wheel of Fate.

In one sense, of course, she has been reborn into a poet whose life and work has caused much debate on literary, social, psychological, spiritual and historical matters. Her work also provided literature with another rebirth: the re-emergence of the self as a fit subject for poetry. For years, poetry had been dominated by TS Eliot and Ezra Pound's 'rules' about the necessity for detachment. Plath developed the freedom to write about the self again and thereby provided a great release of creative energy for modern poets.

Because she had the courage to write about uniquely female experiences such as menstruation, miscarriage, birth, sterility and man-hatred, her work has also provided feminist writers with an impetus to write about previously taboo subjects. As Erica Jong comments,

> Plath sprung open the trap of niceness.. and killed "The Angel In The House" in women's literature once and for all. [2]

BIBLIOGRAPHY

AND

ACKNOWLEDGEMENTS

PRIMARY SOURCES

Sylvia Plath   *Collected Poems*,
                      Faber & Faber, 1981
Sylvia Plath   *Johnny Panic and the Bible of*
                      Dreams, Faber & Faber,1977
                      (Introduction by Ted Hughes)
Sylvia Plath   *Journals,* Smith Collection.
Sylvia Plath   *Letters Home,* Correspondence
                      1950-63,(Ed. Aurelia Schober Plath)
                      Faber and Faber, 1977 Sylvia Plath
                      The Bell Jar, Faber & Faber, 1974

SECONDARY SOURCES

E. Aird   *Sylvia Plath*, Oliver & Boyd, 1973
P. Alexander   *Rough Magic,* Penguin (US only) 1993
A. Alvarez   *The Savage God*, Penguin, 1974
P. Bennett   *My Life a Loaded Gun: Female
                         Creativity and Feminist Politics*,
                         Beacon Press, 1986
P. Blos   *On Adolescence: A Psycho-analytic
                         Interpretation*, Free Press of
                         Glencoe, 1962
L. Bundtzen   *Plath's Incarnations: Woman and
                         The Creative Process*, Ann Arbor,
                         University of Michigan Press, 1983
E. Butscher: Sylvia Plath: The Woman and the
                         Work , Peter Owen, 1979
B. Friedan: *The Feminine Mystique* (Dell) 1972
R. Hayman   *The Death and Life of Sylvia Plath*,
                         Heinemann, 1991
B. Gelpi   A Common Language: The American
                         Woman Poet, essay in *Shakespeare's
                         Sisters: Feminist Essays on Women
                         Poets* edited by S. Gilbert and S. Gubar,
                         Indiana University Press, 1979
R. Graves   *The White Goddess*, Faber &   Faber,
                         1981
R. Hayman   *The Death and Life of Sylvia Plath,*
                         Heinemann, 1991
N.Hunter-Steiner   *A Closer Look at Ariel: A Memory
                         of Sylvia Plath,* Harpers, 1974
E. Jong   Daughters of the New American
                         Revolution, *Sunday Times* 25th
                         April 1978.
J. Kroll   *Chapters in a Mythology: The Poetry
                         of Sylvia Plath*, Harper & Row, 1976

G. Lane (ed.) *Sylvia Plath: New Views on the Poetry,* John Hopkins, University Press, 1979

S. Levine *Who Dies? An Investigation of Conscious Living and Conscious Dying,* Gateway Books, 1988

C. Lukas and H.M. Seiden *Silent Grief: Living in the Wake of Suicide,* Papermac, 1990

A. McLean *The Triple Goddess,* Phanes Press, 1989

C. Matthews *The Elements of the Goddess,* Element Books, 1989

E. Moers *Literary Women,* Women's Press 1978

C. Newman (ed.) *The Art of Sylvia Plath,* Faber & Faber, 1970

J.C. Oates The Death Throes of Romanticism: The Poetry of Sylvia Plath in E. Butscher: *Sylvia Plath: The Woman and The Work,* Peter Owen, 1979

P. Shuttle and P. Redgrove *The Wise Wound: Menstruation and Everywoman,* Paladin,1986

D. Spender *Women Of Ideas,* RKP, 1982

G. Steinem (ed) *First Ms. Reader,* Bantam Books, 1978,

A. Stevenson *Bitter Fame: A Life of Sylvia Plath,* Viking, 1989

M.D. Uroff *Sylvia Plath and Ted Hughes,* University of Illnois Press, 1979

L. Wagner-Martin *Sylvia Plath: A Biography,* Chatto & Windus, 1988

B. Walker *A Woman's Encyclopedia of Myths and Secrets,* Harper & Row, 1983

REFERENCES
& NOTES

Introduction

1. H. Rosenstein, Reconsidering Sylvia Plath, *First Ms. Reader*, Bantam Books 1978, pages 213-214
2. *Longman's English Dictionary*
3. *ibid*
4. "Pursuit", *Collected Poems of Sylvia Plath*, Faber and Faber 1981, page 22, "Ode for Ted", page 29.
5. "Two Sisters of Persephone" ibid. page 31
6. "Kindness" ibid. page 270

Chapter One: Biography

1. L. Ames, Notes Towards A Biography, in C. Newman, *The Art of Sylvia Plath*, Faber & Faber 1970 page 156.
2. Aurelia Plath quoted in L. Wagner- Martin, *Sylvia Plath: A Biography*, Chatto and Windus, 1988, page 20.
3. A. Plath *Letters Home by Sylvia Plath Correspondence 1950-1963*, Faber & Faber, 1977 page 12.
4. Quoted in R. Hayman *The Death & Life of Sylvia Plath*, Heinemann, 1991 page 23.
5. See L. Wagner- Martin *Sylvia Plath: A Biography,* Chatto & Windus, 1988 page 28
6. R Hayman op. cit. page 56.
7. S. Plath *Johnny Panic & The Bible Of Dreams*, Faber & Faber, 1977 page 130
8. L. Ames op. cit. page 166.
9. S. Plath quoted in A. Stevenson *Bitter Fame: A Life Of Sylvia Plath*, Viking 1989, p118.
10. D. Krook, Recollections of Sylvia Plath, in E. Butscher (ed.) *Sylvia Plath: The Woman and the Work*, Peter Owen, 1979 pages 55-56.

Chapter Two: The 1950's

1. B. Friedan: *The Feminine Mystique*, Dell, 1972, page 64
2. Mellon Foundation, Study of Vassar Women, 1956 quoted in Friedan ibid page 143.
3. Peter Blos: *On Adolescence: A Psycho-analytic Interpretation*, Free Press of Glencoe 1962, page 167
4. B. Friedan op.cit. page 116
5. B. Friedan ibid. pages 62-63
6. N. Hunter-Steiner: *A Closer Look at Ariel: A Memory of Sylvia Plath*, Harpers 1973, pages 80-81
7. A. Stevenson: *Bitter Fame: A Life of Sylvia Plath*, Viking 1989, Preface xiii
8. S. Plath *Journals* pages 311-312, Smith Collection.
9. Letter June 1951 quoted in L. Bundtzen *Plath's Incarnations, Women and the Creative Process*, Ann Arbor University of Michigan Press 1983, page 73.
10 N. Hunter Steiner op.cit. page 55
11. D. Spender *Women Of Ideas*, RKP 1982, page 11
12. ibid. page 518

Chapter Three: The Bell Jar

1. S.Plath *The Bell Jar*, Faber and Faber 1963, page 1
2. ibid. page 2
3. ibid. page 4
4. ibid. page 4
5. ibid. page 6
6. ibid. page 6
7. P.Bennett: *My Life A Loaded Gun*, Beacon Press 1986, page 129
8. S. Plath op.cit. page 71
9. S.Plath op.cit. page 80
10. ibid. page 88
11. ibid. page 74
12. ibid. page 88

13. ibid. page 79
14. ibid. page 89
15. ibid. page 122
16. ibid. page 123
17. ibid. page 158
18. ibid. page 213
19. ibid. page 98
20. ibid. page 228
21. ibid. page 235
22. ibid. page 234

Chapter Four: Men

1. T. Hughes "Notes On The Chronological Order of Sylvia Plath's Poetry" in C. Newman: *The Art of Sylvia Plath*, Faber & Faber, 1970 p.191.
2. ibid. p 193
3. Leeds Revolutionary Feminist Group *Political Lesbianism: the Case Against Heterosexuality*, Only Women Press, 1981
4 G. Steiner "Dying Is An Art" in C. Newman op.cit. page 218

Chapter Six: Women

1. James Wood: Who Is Sylvia? *Guardian* 2nd November 1989
2. Letter to Ed. Cohen 1951 quoted in L. Bundtzen, *Plath's Incarnations:Women and the Creative Process*, Ann Arbor University of Michigan Press 1983, page 73
3. N. Hunter-Steiner: *A Closer Look at Ariel: A Memoir of Sylvia Plath*, Harpers 1973, page 76
4. A. Alvarez: *The Savage God*, Penguin 1974, page 28

5. J.C. Oates "The Death Throes of Romanticism: The Poetry of Sylvia Plath" in E.Butscher: *Sylvia Plath: The Woman and the Work* , Peter Owen 1979, page 209

Chapter Seven: Building an Identity - Models for Cultural Victims

1. V. Woolf, "Professions for Women" quoted in E. Moers, *Literary Women*, Women's Press 1978, page 13
2. S. Plath quoted in L. Wagner Martin: *Sylvia Plath:A Life*, Chatto and Windus 1988, page 83
3. M. Atwood quoted in B. Gelpi: *A Common Language: The American Woman Poet* in S. Gilbert and S. Gubar *Shakespeare's Sisters, Feminist Essays On Women Poets*, Indiana University Press 1979, page 270
4. Rampersad "The Ethnic Voice" page 33 quoted in Gelpi ibid. page 270
5. Rampersad ibid. page 35 quoted in Gelpi ibid. page 271.
6. M. Atwood "Survival" page 38 quoted in Gelpi ibid. page 271.

Chapter Eight: Building Identity - Mythology as Poetic Solution

1. A. Mc.Lean: *The Triple Goddess: an Exploration of The Archetypal Feminine*, Phanes Press 1989, page 8
2. C. Matthews *The Elements of The Goddess*, Element Books 1989, page 17
3. A. Mc.Lean op. cit.10
4. P. Shuttle and P. Redgrove: *The Wise Wound: Menstruation and Everywoman*, Paladin 1986

5. R. Graves: *The White Goddess*, Faber & Faber, 1961, page 24
6. ibid.
7. L. Wagner-Martin: *Sylvia Plath: a Biography*, Chatto & Windus 1988, page 141
8. J. Kroll *Chapters in a Mythology: The Poetry of Sylvia Plath*, Harper & Row, 1976, page 223, Note 35
9. R. Graves op.cit. page 446-447
10. ibid page 449
11. J. Kroll op.cit. page 224 Note 34
12. B. Walker: *A Woman's Encyclopedia of Myths and Secrets,* Harper and Row 1983, page 877
13. J. Kroll op.cit. page 125
14. ibid. page 66
15. A. Alvarez *The Savage God,*Penguin 1974, page 22
16. R. Graves op.cit. page 194
17. B. Walker op.cit. pages 847-848
18. ibid. page 452
19. J. Kroll op.cit. pages 206-207

Chapter Nine: Afterlife

1. L. Wagner-Martin, *Sylvia Plath: A Biography,* Chatto & Windus, 1988, frontispiece.
2. S. Levine *Who Dies?: An Investigation of Conscious Living and Conscious Dying,* Gateway Books 1988, page 216.
3. A. Alvarez *The Savage God,* Penguin 1974, page 23.
4. R. Hayman *The Death and Life of Sylvia Plath,* Heinemann 1991, page 184
5. A. Stevenson, *Bitter Fame: A Life of Sylvia Plath,* Viking Penguin 1989, pages 283-4
6. R. Hayman op.cit. page 15
7   A. Stevenson op.cit. page 286

8.   A. Alvarez "Sylvia Plath" in C. Newman (ed.) *The Art of Sylvia Plath*, Faber & Faber, 1970, page 67
9.   I. Howe "The Plath Celebration: A Partial Dissent" in E. Butscher (ed.) *Sylvia Plath: The Woman And The Work*, Peter Owen 1979, pages 225-237.
10. Robin Morgan, *Monster*, a poem not published in Britain and privately circulated within Women's Groups in the 1970's.
11. A. Stevenson op. cit. page 301
12. R. Hayman op.cit. page 187
13. A. Stevenson op. cit. page 287
14. P. Alexander "In Search of the Complete Plath" in the *Weekend Guardian* 1st August 1992
15. ibid.
16. Ted. Hughes in Introduction to *Sylvia Plath Johnny Panic and The Bible Of Dreams*, Faber and Faber, 1977, page 11
17. R. Hayman op.cit. page 189
18   Ted Hughes op.cit. page 19
19   C. Lukas and H. Seiden *Silent Grief: Living In The Wake of Suicide*, Papermac 1990, Chapter 2 of this excellent study of the survivors of suicide deals with emotional reactions to and consequences of living with a suicide in one's life. The authors, using extensive medical evidence, state that suicide survivors suffer from Post-traumatic Stress Disorder. This is the term now applied to the survivors of major disasters and is equivalent to shell shock or battle neurosis.
20. R. Hayman op.cit. page 13
21   C. Lukas and H. Seiden op.cit. page 53
22. ibid. Chapter 2. I also have personal experience which seems relevant here. As mentioned in the Preface my father committed suicide. Soon after his death my mother burned all photographs which she had of him. I have tried to obtain a photograph of him for several years. Several relatives I've asked have disclosed that they too (without knowing of my mother's actions) had destroyed their photographs of him.
23. R. Hayman op.cit. pages 187 - 8.

24. ibid.
25. ibid.
26. P. Alexander op.cit.
27 ibid.
28. E. Butscher "In Search of Sylvia: An Introduction" in
Sylvia Plath: The Woman and the Work, Peter Owen
1979, page13.
29. ibid.
30. ibid. page 3
31. R. Hayman op.cit. page 193
32. P. Alexander ibid.
33. ibid.
34. ibid.
35. ibid.
36. ibid.
37. ibid.
38. A. Stevenson op.cit. page ix
39. Since the first printing of this book, I have met Anne
Stevenson. I realised during this meeting that she is losing
her hearing - this explains her apparent evasion of questions
at the York Study Day.
40. Sylvia Plath quoted in L. Wagner-Martin op.cit.
page 247

Conclusion

1.   Parasuicide is the term used by psychiatrists to
describe suicide attempts, nearly always made by women,
that are not intended to succeed. Parasuicide usually
involves self-poisoning. Alvarez, in *The Savage God*, makes
a very convincing case for the idea that Plath's death was in
this category. See pages 49 - 53.
2.   Erica Jong quoted in "Daughters of the New American
Revolution" *Sunday Times* article 25th. April 1978.

INDEX

141

Other Books from Pennine Pens

○ A Little Bridge
Debjani Chatterjee,
Simon Fletcher
Basir Sultan Kazmi
To mark the 50th anniversary of the independence of India and Pakistan, these three talented Northern poets have collaborated in a collection of poems which reflects the connections between the cultures of Britain and the Indian sub-continent. Director of the Poetry Society, Chris Meade has written the forward, describing the poems as "excellent" and a "wondrous fusion" of the different cultures. (£5.95)

http://www.penpens.demon.co.uk/books/alb.html   ISBN 1 873378 77 7

○ The Chess Board by Basir Sultan Kazmi
A play in four acts, was originally published in Pakistan (1987) and was widely appreciated. Set in olden times, the princess will only marry someone who can beat her at chess. Son of a famous Urdu poet, the late Nasir Kazmi, Basir Kazmi has now been translated into English. Basir Kazmi's work has already been used as GCSE coursework and we are confident that this play will find a good home in many class-rooms. (£4.95)   http://www.penpens.demon.co.uk/books/chess.html   ISBN 1 873378 27 0

○ The Occasions of Love by Simon Fletcher
The Occasions of Love celebrates all the experiences and emotions of love: discovery, pleasure, loss and isolation in a softly erotic, elegant, consistently witty and often ironic way. *I enjoyed the deft fluency, the economy, the pure tone, the 'pang' - (as Frost said 'no pang, no poem').* **Ted Hughes**
(£4.95)   http://www.penpens.demon.co.uk/books/occasions.html   ISBN 1 873378 07 6

○ The Occasions of Love: **Audio book version** (£4.95)

○ Cycling in Search of the Cathars
Chris Ratcliffe and Elaine Connell
The Cathars were vegetarian, pacifist, recognised women priests, believed in reincarnation and were against marriage and the feudal system of medieval, southwest France. The Church sent crusades to attack them and created the Inquisition to persecute them. This is the story of an historical investigation carried out by bicycle in the foothills of the Pyrenees into what some have described as the "Buddhists of the West". This book about the "heretics" of medieval southwest France is **currently out of print**. A full colour **digital book on CD** is, however, available for PCs and Macs. (£9.95)   http://www.penpens.demon.co.uk/books/cat.html   ISBN 1 87337 00 9

✪ Me, Mick and M31 by Andrew Bibby
Children's environmental mystery: there is something mysterious about Molly's new next-door neighbour. Why does she have a big pink van which advertises pizzas? Where does she drive off to late at night? And what has this to do with a strange organisation called Fight the Light, with its instructions to "keep watching M31"? Molly and her friend Mick decide to find out. Their efforts lead to a series of night-time adventures and to their discovery of an unusual environmental campaign. An exciting and enjoyable story - especially for anyone who likes pizzas...Andrew Bibby is a writer and journalist whose work appears regularly in *The Independent, The Observer* and a wide range of other national publications. The book is illustrated by **Sean Creagh.**
(£5.95)   http://www.penpens.demon.co.uk/books/m31.html   ISBN 1 873378 12 2

✪ Teaching Pack for Mick, Me and M31
Elaine Connell has written a highly acclaimed teaching pack for Andrew Bibby's book, consisting of 45 worksheets, differentiated to include work for students with ability and special needs. This is inclusive with orders for sets of *Me, Mick and M31* books or may be bought separately for £15 or is inclusive with a set of books.

✪ Presenting the Past: Anne Lister of Halifax - Jill Liddington
Anne Lister - scholar, heiress and traveller - owned and ran the Shibden Hall estate in Halifax. Her four-million word diaries give a vivid picture of the daily life of an independent woman in the early nineteenth century. In *Presenting the Past,* Jill Liddington tells the dramatic story of how the diaries and letters have survived since Anne Lister's death in 1840. She recounts how the code, in which Anne recorded her lesbian affairs in her journals, was eventually deciphered. (£5.95 and 65p p&p)
http://www.penpens.demon.co.uk/books/al.html   ISBN 1 873378 02 5

✪ Asma's Egg
Words: Chris Ratcliffe. Illustrations: Sean Creagh
For children 4-7   (£1.95 and 45p p&p)
http://www.penpens.demon.co.uk/books/asma.html

✪ Poppies

A collection of poems by Elaine Connell   (£1.95)

*All Pennine Pens books are available from bookshops and
online at http://www.penpens.demon.co.uk*